Our "Compacted" Compact Clinicals Team

Dear Valued Customer,

Welcome to Compact Clinicals. We are committed to bringing mental health professionals up-to-date diagnostic and treatment information in a compact, timesaving, easy-to-read format. Our line of books provides current, thorough reviews of assessment and treatment strategies for mental disorders. These books will help each practitioner more effectively plan treatment interventions.

We've "compacted" complete information for diagnosing each disorder and comparing how different theoretical orientations approach treatment. Our books use nonacademic language, real-world examples, and well-defined terminology.

Enjoy this and other timesaving books from Compact Clinicals.

Sincerely,

Melanie A Dean

Melanie Dean, Ph.D.
President

D1299452

Compact Clinicals New Line of Books

Compact Clinicals currently offers these condensed reviews for professionals:

- **Aggressive & Defiant Behavior:** *The Latest Assessment and Treatment Strategies for the Conduct Disorders*

- **Attention Deficit Hyperactivity Disorder (in Adults and Children):** *The Latest Assessment and Treatment Strategies*

- **Borderline Personality Disorder:** *The Latest Assessment and Treatment Strategies*

- **Depression in Adults:** *The Latest Assessment and Treatment Strategies*

- **Obsessive Compulsive Disorder:** *The Latest Assessment and Treatment Strategies*

- **Post Traumatic Stress Disorder:** *The Latest Assessment and Treatment Strategies*

Call for Writers

Compact Clinicals is always interested in publishing new titles in order to keep our selection of books current and comprehensive. If you have a book proposal or an idea you would like to discuss, please call or write to:

Melanie Dean, Ph.D., President
Compact Clinicals
7205 NW Waukomis Suite A
Kansas City, MO 64151
(816) 587-0044

Aggressive and Defiant Behavior

The Latest Assessment and Treatment Strategies for the Conduct Disorders

Second Edition

by
J. Mark Eddy, Ph.D.

First Edition Titled — Conduct Disorders: The Latest Assessment and Treatment Strategies (1996)

CC Compact Clinicals...*condensed reviews for professionals*

This book is intended solely for use by properly trained and licensed mental health professionals, who already possess a solid education in psychological theory, research, and treatment. This book is in no way intended to replace or supplement such training and education, nor is it to be used as the sole basis for any decision regarding treatment. It is merely intended to be used by such trained and educated professionals as a review and resource guide when considering how to best treat a person with a Conduct Disorder.

Aggressive and Defiant Behaviors
The Latest Assessment and Treatment Strategies for the Conduct Disorders
Second Edition

by
J. Mark Eddy, Ph.D.

First Edition Titled — Conduct Disorders: The Latest Assessment and Treatment Strategies

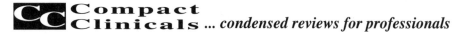 **Compact Clinicals** ... *condensed reviews for professionals*

Published by: Compact Clinicals
                  7205 NW Waukomis Dr., Suite A
                  Kansas City, MO. 64151
                  816-587-0044
Copyright © 2001 Dean Psych Press Corp., d/b/a Compact Clinicals

Content Editing by:
        Melanie A. Dean, Ph.D.
Copy Editing by:
        InCredible English
        P.O. Box 1309
        Salt Lake City, UT 84091
DeskTop Publishing by:
        Cactus Tracks
        1958 Five Iron Drive
        Castle Rock, CO 80104
Cover Design by:
        Patrick G. Handley

Library of Congress Cataloging in Publication Data
Eddy, J. Mark
    Aggressive and Defiant Behavior: the latest assessment and treatment strategies for the conduct disorders/by J. Mark Eddy.
    p. ;cm.
    Rev. ed. of: Conduct disorders. c1996.
    Includes bibliographical references and index.
    ISBN 1-887537-15-5 (pbk.)
        1. Conduct disorders in children. 2. Conduct disorders in adolescence. 3. Conduct disorders in children--Treatment. 4 Conduct disorders in adolescence--Treatment. I. Eddy, J. Mark. Conduct disorders. II. Title.
        [DNLM: 1. Conduct Disorder--diagnosis--Adolescence. 2. Conduct Disorder--diagnosis--Child. 3. Aggression--Adolescence. 4. Agression--Child. 5. Conduct Disorder--therapy--Adolescence. 6. Conduct Disorder--therapy--Child. WS 350.6 E21a2001]
    RJ506.C65E33 2001
    618.92'858206--dc21
                                                        00-052311
ISBN:1-887537-15-5

10 9 8 7 6 5 4 3 2 1

Read Me First

As a mental health professional, often the information you need can only be obtained after countless hours of reading or library research. If your schedule precludes this time commitment, Compact Clinicals is the answer.

Our books are practitioner oriented with easy-to-read treatment descriptions and examples. Compact Clinicals books are written in a nonacademic style. Our books are formatted to make the first reading as well as ongoing reference quick and easy. You will find:

- *Anecdotes*—Each chapter begins and ends with a fictionalized account that personalizes the disorder. These accounts include a "**Dear Diary**" entry at the beginning of each chapter that illustrates a typical client's viewpoint about their disorder. Each chapter ends with "**File Notes**" of a fictional therapist, Pat Owen. These "**File Notes**" address assessment, diagnosis, and treatment considerations for the client writing the "**Dear Diary**" entries.

- *Sidebars*—Columns on the outside of each page highlight important information, preview upcoming sections or concepts, and define terms used in the text.

- *Definitions*—Terms are defined in the sidebars where they originally appear in the text and in an alphabetical glossary on pages 75 through 76.

- *References*—Numbered references appear in the text following information from that source. Full references appear in a bibliography on pages 77 through 86.

- *Case Examples*—Our examples illustrate typical client comments or conversational exchanges that help clarify different treatment approaches. Identifying information in the examples (e.g., the individual's real name, profession, age, and/or location) has been changed to protect the confidentiality of those clients discussed in case examples.

Contents

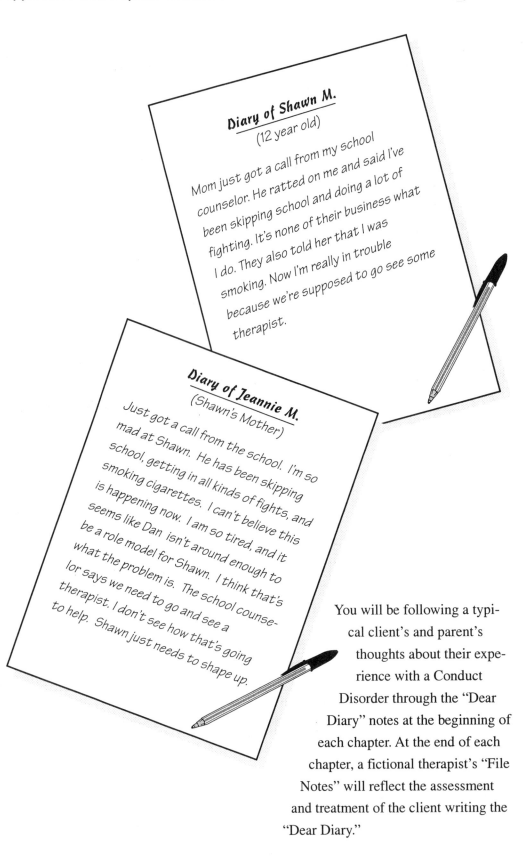

Diary of Shawn M.
(12 year old)

Mom just got a call from my school counselor. He ratted on me and said I've been skipping school and doing a lot of fighting. It's none of their business what I do. They also told her that I was smoking. Now I'm really in trouble because we're supposed to go see some therapist.

Diary of Jeannie M.
(Shawn's Mother)

Just got a call from the school. I'm so mad at Shawn. He has been skipping school, getting in all kinds of fights, and smoking cigarettes. I can't believe this is happening now. I am so tired, and it seems like Dan isn't around enough to be a role model for Shawn. I think that's what the problem is. The school counselor says we need to go and see a therapist. I don't see how that's going to help. Shawn just needs to shape up.

You will be following a typical client's and parent's thoughts about their experience with a Conduct Disorder through the "Dear Diary" notes at the beginning of each chapter. At the end of each chapter, a fictional therapist's "File Notes" will reflect the assessment and treatment of the client writing the "Dear Diary."

Chapter One: Overview of the Conduct Disorders

The "conduct disorders" are considered one of the most expensive child mental health issues in the United States today, reflecting how often these children and their parents come in contact with numerous social service professionals. This intensive service utilization commonly involves physicians and other emergency room personnel, school counselors, police officers, judges, and juvenile justice system staff.[1,2]

While recent school shootings in rural and suburban areas have sharply focused attention on youth crime and violence, child antisocial behavior in the United States is not new.[3] For decades, children and adolescents displaying troublesome patterns of antisocial behavior have accounted for almost half of all referrals to child mental health clinics.[1,4] Such behavior patterns usually include some combination of chronic disobedience, aggression, temper tantrums, lying, and stealing. The outcomes of the most severe of these behaviors may include physical injury, disability, or death; emotional injury; and/or property damage or loss. Given these serious outcomes, the consequences of child conduct problems reflect a critical social problem in the United States.

What Are the Conduct Disorders?

Clinicians use the term "conduct disorder" to describe a persistent pattern of child antisocial behaviors that violate fundamental social rules and/or the basic rights of others. Conduct-disordered behaviors include:

- Aggression to people or animals

- Destruction of property

- Deceitfulness or theft

- Serious violations of rules

- Negativistic, hostile, or defiant behavior

Most children exhibit some antisocial behaviors at various times during their development. For example, disobedience and temper tantrums are normative behaviors during childhood. To warrant a conduct disorder diagnosis, a child must display a variety of antisocial behaviors to a *clinically significant* degree.

This chapter answers the following:

- **What are the Conduct Disorders?**—This section presents the six different diagnoses used to categorize child antisocial behaviors.

- **How Common are the Conduct Disorders?**—This section presents prevalence rates among children and adolescents.

- **What is the Prognosis for those with a Conduct Disorder?**—This section highlights research on whether or not children with Conduct Disorders will continue experiencing symptoms through adolescence and into adulthood.

clinically significant—*a pattern of behavioral or psychological symptoms that has become established enough, severe enough, and impairing enough to interfere with a child's day-to-day functioning in one or more settings (i.e., home, school, community)*

In this book, "conduct disorders" will refer to the six different diagnoses given for ongoing patterns of child antisocial behaviors by the <u>Diagnostic and Statistical Manual of Mental Disorders</u>—Fourth Edition (DSM-IV).[5] These diagnoses are:

- Conduct Disorder (CD)

- Oppositional Defiant Disorder (ODD)

- Disruptive Behavior Disorder Not Otherwise Specified (DBD-NOS)

- Adjustment Disorder: With Mixed Disturbance of Emotions and Conduct

- Adjustment Disorder: With Disturbance of Conduct

- Child or Adolescent Antisocial Behavior

How Common are the Conduct Disorders?

Currently, there are from two to six percent of children and adolescents exhibiting a conduct disorder in the U.S.[2] Prevalence rates for conduct disorders vary depending on age, sex, and geographical location.[6-10]

- ***Age*** — Across childhood, prevalence rates vary as follows:

    - Elementary school: 2 percent of girls and 7 percent of boys[6]

    - Middle school: 2 to 10 percent of girls and 3 to 16 percent of boys[7-9]

    - High school: 4 to 15 percent of boys and girls[6,9,10]

In studies directly comparing rates across age groups, the prevalence of conduct disorders increases as children reach adolescence.[8,9]

- ***Gender***— Studies that compare boys and girls across age groups indicate that prevalence rates are more equal between the sexes during middle to late adolescence than during early childhood.[8-10]

- ***Geographical Location*** — Rates are higher for younger children from urban areas than from rural areas. However, rates are similar for adolescents in urban and rural areas.[6,11]

What is the Prognosis for those with a Conduct Disorder?

One of the strongest predictors of current child antisocial behavior is previous child antisocial behavior.[12-15] However, this prediction is not as strong as was previously thought. Only about 50 percent of children who display antisocial behaviors during elementary school continue to do so during adolescence, and only 40 to 75 percent of adolescents who display antisocial behavior continue such behaviors as adults.[16-18]

Several risk factors increase the chance that an elementary school-aged child displaying conduct-disordered behaviors will continue to during adolescence and adulthood.[20-21] These factors are:

- Displaying hyperactive, impulsive, and/or inattentive behaviors (e.g., difficulty paying attention and sitting still in the classroom)

- Having an early onset of antisocial behaviors (i.e., before or during early adolescence)

- Committing many different types of antisocial behaviors (e.g., lies, cheats, steals, and fights)

- Exhibiting a high frequency of antisocial behaviors (e.g., gets in many fights)

- Displaying antisocial behaviors in multiple settings (e.g., fights at home, during school, and on the neighborhood playground)

These risk factors are interrelated. For example, children who exhibit hyperactive behaviors are more likely to have an early onset of antisocial behaviors.[22] Children with early onset of antisocial behaviors tend to commit more frequent antisocial behaviors.[23] Those who commit more frequent antisocial behaviors are more likely to commit violent acts.[24]

Of all the risk factors, age of onset seems to be the most important. Several researchers have hypothesized that children who do not begin to exhibit antisocial behaviors until adolescence are less likely to continue such behaviors into adulthood. In contrast, children who begin their antisocial "careers" during elementary school are most at risk for conduct-disordered problems as adults.[25,26]

Support for the early onset hypothesis is strong. The average age of antisocial behavior onset for adults diagnosed with Antisocial Personality Disorder (the adult equivalent of CD) is age eight or nine.[27] Further, only about 10 percent of individuals who did not exhibit antisocial behaviors during childhood and adolescence begin to do so during adulthood.[28] Studies of adults who displayed child antisocial behaviors at a young age (versus those who did not) indicate that the early starters:[17,21,29,30]

- Commit more acts of murder, rape, robbery, and arson
- Are more likely to commit multiple offenses
- Are more likely to be incarcerated

Adolescent girls with conduct problems are more likely to become mothers at a very young age, be single parents, and have children that display early signs of psychosocial problems, including conduct-disordered behavior.[34]

Although many adults who displayed frequent antisocial behaviors as children do not commit criminal acts as adults, they often suffer other significant impairments.[31] Studies have linked a history of childhood conduct problems to adult alcoholism, psychiatric problems, marital problems, poor work performance, and poor physical health.[15,17,19,29,30,32,33] Each of these problems can disrupt the ability of a parent to effectively discipline and monitor their children. In turn, such disruption increases the likelihood that the child of a parent with a childhood history of severe antisocial behavior will exhibit conduct problems.[19,35]

Therapy Notes from the Desk of Pat Owen

Saw a mother, Jeannie, and her 12 yr. old son Shawn, for the first time today. According to Mother, Shawn has been skipping school, fighting, stealing, smoking cigarettes, and getting poor grades. Mother is uncertain when these behaviors started, but Shawn reports that many of these activities have been going on for at least two years. Mother reports that Shawn has been angry and defiant for quite a while now. Mother divorced Shawn's biological father when Shawn was 5. Stepfather (Dan) travels on business frequently. Mother reports that Dan tries to get involved when at home. Recommend collecting further information from Mother, Dan, and teachers.

Chapter Two: Diagnosing the Conduct Disorders

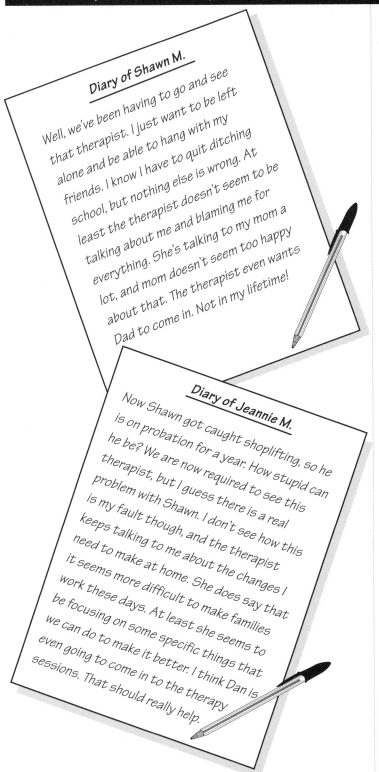

Diary of Shawn M.

Well, we've been having to go and see that therapist. I just want to be left alone and be able to hang with my friends. I know I have to quit ditching school, but nothing else is wrong. At least the therapist doesn't seem to be talking about me and blaming me for everything. She's talking to my mom a lot, and mom doesn't seem too happy about that. The therapist even wants Dad to come in. Not in my lifetime!

Diary of Jeannie M.

Now Shawn got caught shoplifting, so he is on probation for a year. How stupid can he be? We are now required to see this therapist, but I guess there is a real problem with Shawn. I don't see how this is my fault though, and the therapist keeps talking to me about the changes I need to make at home. She does say that it seems more difficult to make families work these days. At least she seems to be focusing on some specific things that we can do to make it better. I think Dan is even going to come in to the therapy sessions. That should really help.

This chapter answers the following:

- **What Criteria are Used to Diagnose the Conduct Disorders?**—This section presents DSM-IV criteria for the six diagnoses that relate to child antisocial behaviors.

- **How do Children with CD Present During Initial Office Evaluations?**—This section discusses symptoms presented by those with one of the Conduct Disorders.

- **How Can Clinicians Develop an Effective Assessment Strategy?**—This section presents a process for developing an assessment strategy and implementation plan.

- **What Other Disorders Commonly Occur with Conduct Disorders?**—This section discusses co-occurring disorders.

What Criteria are Used to Diagnose Conduct Disorders?

Information gathered during assessment determines the treatment plan developed for a given child.

Only one of the six diagnoses can be made at any given point. The order of precedence for the DSM-IV child antisocial behavior disorders is:

1. CD
2. ODD
3. DBD-NOS
4. Adjustment Disorder (mixed)
5. Adjustment Disorder (conduct)
6. Child or Adolescent Antisocial Behavior

In DSM-IV, child antisocial behaviors are categorized into six diagnoses (five of which are considered mental disorders). Only one diagnosis can be made at a time.[36] These diagnoses are:

- **Conduct Disorder** — Conduct Disorder (CD) categorizes an ongoing pattern of behaviors that clearly violates the rights of others or disregards the accepted rules of home, school, and/or community. For example, during the past six months, Jake frequently bullied and threatened others, initiated physical fights, and used a knife during several of those fights. The major CD behavior types are aggression towards people or animals, destruction of property, lying and stealing, and rule-breaking.

- **Oppositional Defiant Disorder** — Oppositional Defiant Disorder (ODD) categorizes an ongoing pattern of child behaviors that are defiant and hostile towards others, particularly toward authority figures. For example, over the past year, Meghan frequently lost her temper, became angry, argued, and refused to cooperative with her parents and teachers.

- **Disruptive Behavior Disorder-Not Otherwise Specified** — Disruptive Behavior Disorder-Not Otherwise Specified (DBD-NOS) categorizes an ongoing pattern of CD and/or ODD behaviors that fail to meet the criteria for a CD or ODD diagnosis. For example, during the past six months, Chris frequently initiated fights, argued with adults, and defied adult requests. He reportedly demonstrated no other CD or ODD symptoms.

- **Adjustment Disorder with Mixed Disturbance of Emotions and Conduct** — This **Adjustment Disorder** categorizes antisocial behaviors and emotional symptoms that begin within three months **of an identifiable psychosocial stressor** (e.g., moving into a high-crime neighborhood, parental conflict). Further, the symptoms do not meet criteria for one of the previously mentioned disorders. For example, Joey has intense mood swings and fights frequently with schoolmates, with the mood swings and fighting commencing within a month following his father's death.

- **Adjustment Disorder with Disturbance of Conduct** — An Adjustment Disorder characterized by antisocial behaviors only.

- ***Child or Adolescent Antisocial Behavior*** — Child or Adolescent Antisocial Behavior categorizes isolated antisocial behaviors that are not considered indicative of a *mental disorder.* For example, Chris shoplifted three times during the past six months, but apparently exhibited no other CD or ODD symptoms.

According to DSM-IV, CD can be diagnosed if the specified criteria are met whether or not other psychiatric diagnoses exist.[3] The same is true of ODD except when the symptoms occur exclusively in the presence of a diagnosed Mood Disorder or a Psychotic Disorder. When this occurs, the clinician should assume that the oppositional behaviors are part of the constellation of symptoms of the Mood or Psychotic Disorders, rather than representative of ODD.

mental disorder—a clinically significant pattern of behavioral or psychological symptoms associated with one or more major negative outcomes (e.g., distress, pain, injury, disability, confinement)

Figure 2.1 — DSM-IV Diagnostic Criteria

I. 312.8 Conduct Disorder

A. A repetitive and persistent pattern of behavior in which the basic rights of others or major age-appropriate societal norms or rules are violated as manifested by the presence of three (or more) of the following criteria in the past 12 months, with at least one criterion present in the past six months:

Aggression to people and animals

(1) often bullies, threatens, or intimidates others

(2) often initiates physical fights

(3) has used a weapon that can cause serious physical harm to others (e.g., a bat, brick, broken bottle, knife, gun)

(4) has been physically cruel to people

(5) has been physically cruel to animals

(6) has stolen while confronting a victim (e.g., mugging, purse snatching, extortion, armed robbery)

(7) has forced someone into sexual activity

Destruction of property

(8) has deliberately engaged in fire setting with the intention of causing serious damage

(9) has deliberately destroyed others' property (other than by fire setting)

Deceitfulness or theft

(10) has broken into someone else's house, building, or car

(11) often lies to obtain goods or favors or to avoid obligations (i.e., "cons" others)

(12) has stolen items of nontrivial value without confronting a victim (e.g., shoplifting, but without breaking and entering; forgery)

Serious violations of rules

(13) often stays out at night despite parental prohibitions, beginning before age 13 years

(14) has run away from home overnight at least twice while living in parental or parental surrogate home (or once without returning for a lengthy period)

(15) is often truant from school, beginning before age 13 years

B. The disturbance in behavior causes clinically significant impairment in social, academic, or occupational functioning

Continued on Page 8

C. If the individual is age 18 years or older, criteria are not met for Antisocial Personality Disorder

Specify type based on age of onset:

Childhood-Onset Type: onset of at least one criterion characteristic of Conduct Disorder prior to age 10 years

Adolescent-Onset Type: absence of any criteria characteristic of Conduct Disorder prior to age 10 years

Specify severity:

Mild: few if any conduct problems in excess of those required to make the diagnosis **and** conduct problems cause only minor harm to others

Moderate: number of conduct problems and effect on others intermediate between "mild" and "severe"

Severe: many conduct problems in excess of those required to make the diagnosis **or** conduct problems cause considerable harm to others

II. 313.81 Oppositional Defiant Disorder

A. A pattern of negativistic, hostile, and defiant behavior lasting at least six months, during which four (or more) of the following are present:

  (1) often loses temper

  (2) often argues with adults

  (3) often actively defies or refuses to comply with adults' requests or rules

  (4) often deliberately annoys people

  (5) often blames others for his or her mistakes or misbehavior

  (6) is often touchy or easily annoyed by others

  (7) is often angry and resentful

  (8) is often spiteful or vindictive

    Note: Consider a criterion met only if the behavior occurs more frequently than is typically observed in individuals of comparable age and developmental level.

B. The disturbance in behavior causes clinically significant impairment in social, academic, or occupational functioning.

C. The behaviors do not occur exclusively during the course of a Psychotic or Mood Disorder.

D. Criteria are not met for Conduct Disorder, and, if the individual is age 18 years or older, criteria are not met for Antisocial Personality Disorder.

III. 312.9 Disruptive Behavior Disorder Not Otherwise Specified

This category is for disorders characterized by conduct or oppositional defiant behaviors that do not meet the criteria for Conduct Disorder or Oppositional Defiant Disorder. For example, include clinical presentations that do not meet full criteria for Oppositional Defiant Disorder or Conduct Disorder, but in which there is clinically significant impairment.

IV. 309.4 Adjustment Disorder: With Mixed Disturbance of Emotions and Conduct

A. The development of emotional or behavioral symptoms in response to an identifiable stressor(s) occurring within three months of the onset of the stressor(s).

B. These symptoms or behaviors are clinically significant as evidenced by either of the following:

  (1) marked distress in excess of what would be expected from exposure to the stressor

  (2) significant impairment in social or occupational (academic) functioning

C. The stress-related disturbance does not meet the criteria for another specific Axis I disorder and is not merely an exacerbation of a preexisting Axis I or Axis II disorder.

D. The symptoms do not represent bereavement.

E. Once the stressor (or its consequences) has terminated, the symptoms do not persist for more than an additional six months.

Specify if:

Acute: if the disturbance lasts less than six months

Chronic: if the disturbance lasts for six months or longer

Continued on Page 9

This subtype should be used when the predominant manifestations are both emotional symptoms (e.g., depression, anxiety) and a disturbance of conduct (see above subtype).

V. 309.3 Adjustment Disorder: With Disturbance of Conduct

Criteria A through E above and:

This subtype should be used when the predominant manifestation is a disturbance in conduct in which there is violation of the rights of others or of major age-appropriate societal norms and rules (e.g., truancy, vandalism, reckless driving, fighting, defaulting on legal responsibilities).

VI. V71.02 Child or Adolescent Antisocial Behavior

This category can be used when the focus of clinical attention is antisocial behavior in a child or adolescent that is not due to a mental disorder (e.g., Conduct Disorder or an Impulse-Control Disorder). Examples include isolated antisocial acts of children or adolescents (not a pattern of antisocial behavior).

(Reprinted with permission from the American Psychiatric Association: Diagnostic and Statistical Manual of Mental Disorders, Fourth Edition. Washington, DC, American Psychiatric Association, 1994.)

Diagnostic Clarifying Information

Clinical Significance

When diagnosing a child with a conduct disorder, the clinician must decide whether a pattern of antisocial behaviors has become established enough, severe enough, and impairing enough to be labeled *clinically significant*. Impairment is probably most crucial to the idea of clinical significance; the maladaptive behaviors that qualify the child for a conduct disorder diagnosis should significantly interfere with the child's day-to-day functioning in one or more settings (i.e., home, school, and community).

Specific Criteria

The symptom "often stays out at night despite parental prohibitions, beginning before age 13" is an example of a cluster of behaviors dubbed *"wandering."*[37] Wandering (or conversely, a lack of *"monitoring"*) is strongly predictive of child antisocial behavior.[13,37,38] In DSM-IV, wandering in spite of parental rules is no longer considered a predictor of antisocial behavior, but rather a conduct-disordered behavior in its own right.

The symptom, "often bullies, threatens, or intimidates others" presents the symptoms in a way that might better apply to girls exhibiting CD. Researchers have hypothesized that girls

Making any psychiatric diagnosis is a subjective process: the clinician must decide that a child, relative to his or her peers, is behaving in ways that are deviant enough to warrant a psychiatric label.

clinically significant—a pattern of behavioral or psychological symptoms that have become established enough, severe enough, and impairing enough to interfere with a child's day-to-day functioning in one or more settings (i.e., home, school, community)

wandering — child spends time in unstructured, adult-unsupervised settings

monitoring — hour-to-hour each day, parent knows who their child is with, where their child is and what their child is doing

*relational aggression —
harm perpetrated against
others using indirect, non-
physical means such as
manipulation, threats,
and exclusion.*

*The age of 10 years is not
an empirically validated
number. It is used in the
DSM-IV to mark the line
between the "early" and
"late" starter groups, and is
somewhere between age 10
and 15 years.*

*deviant peer groups —
friendship groups comprising children who have
difficulty with falling grades,
engage in illegal activities,
and have little contact with
prosocial activities*

*As discussed in the Behavior
Therapy section of Chapter 3
(pages 30-44), deviant peer
groups appear to play a
central role in the development and maintenance of child
antisocial behavior, particularly during adolescence.*

tend to use *"relational aggression,"* such as intimidation and threatening, more than boys.[36,39] However, at present, there exists scant data to support this hypothesis.

Early and Late Subtypes

The focus on "early" (defined as onset before age 10), and "late" (defined as onset at age 10 or older), subtypes is based on research indicating that children who exhibit antisocial behaviors during preschool and elementary school are at a high risk for continuing to behave antisocially as adults.[21] Research-ers hypothesize that "early starters" learn their behavioral rep-ertoires first through social interactions in the home, and later through their social interactions at school and with peers. In contrast, researchers hypothesize that children who begin to exhibit antisocial behaviors during middle school and high school learn many of these behaviors within *deviant peer groups*. These older children are more likely to discontinue their antisocial behaviors prior to adulthood.[25,26] Some research findings support both the early- and later-starter hypotheses.[40,41]

Using the Disruptive Behavior Disorder-NOS Diagnosis

The diagnosis, Disruptive Behavior Disorder-Not Otherwise Specified (DBD-NOS) allows clinicians the discretion to diag-nose those children who do not meet the criteria for CD or ODD, but **do** display some clinically significant behaviors. Children who display a few mild ODD behaviors or a few more serious ODD and/or CD symptoms could be categorized as DBD-NOS. For example, a child who consistently steals and lies, but commits no other CD or ODD behaviors, could receive a DBD-NOS diagnosis.

This diagnosis should be used when CD or ODD cannot be diagnosed and the following three conditions are present:

1. The behaviors seem to reflect a consistent pattern of anti-social behaviors

2. The behaviors persist over time (i.e., at least six months)

3. The behaviors result in clinically significant impairment in the home, in the school, or in the community.

How do Children with CD Present During Initial Office Evaluations?

How children, who are ultimately diagnosed with a conduct disorder, present themselves in the clinician's office can vary dramatically. Some children may be withdrawn, hostile, and minimally cooperative (e.g., giving one-word answers to questions). Others may act shy, cling to a parent, speak minimally, and refuse to engage in activities with the clinician. Still, others may be quite restless and inattentive. Much to the consternation of their exasperated parents, some children who are quite non-compliant at home may comply quite readily with the demands placed on them by the clinician.

Just as children who display conduct-disordered behaviors can behave differently during an interview than they do during their everyday activities, their behavioral repertoires at home, at school, and in the community may be strikingly different from each other. Thus, to adequately assess conduct-disorder symptoms, clinicians must investigate how children behave in each key setting. The easiest way to do this is to ask the opinions of the adults who spend a significant amount of time in each setting. Unfortunately, adult reports of child behaviors are affected by factors other than true behavioral variation.[44,45] The current emotional state or the past experiences of adults may change, or bias, the way they perceive the child's behavior.

For example, some adults may see behaviors as aversive or deviant when other adults would rate the same behaviors as neutral. In a series of studies on bias, mothers of children exhibiting antisocial behavior problems and mothers of children with no behavior problems were shown videotapes of other parents interacting with their own child. The mothers were asked to rate selected child behaviors on the tapes as either *prosocial*, neutral, or deviant. Mothers of children exhibiting problem behaviors tended to classify a greater number of child behaviors as "deviant" than either independent observers or mothers of children not exhibiting problem behaviors.[46,47]

Whatever behaviors clinicians observe during intake, there is no evidence that the information gained from such observations reliably assists in diagnosing a valid conduct disorder.

Although some children with a conduct disorder do exhibit challenging behaviors, many do not misbehave during initial office evaluations.[42,43]

prosocial—responsible, socially considerate behavior

How Can Clinicians Develop an Assessment Strategy?

The most effective way to overcome the specific biases of various raters and to reliably map out a child's behavioral repertoire is to simultaneously consider multiple points of view.

Developing an Assessment Strategy

Assessment does not end at the beginning of treatment, but is used to monitor the progress of treatment.

Assessing a child from multiple vantage points provides clinicians with a more reliable, valid picture of a child's current functioning and environment. At the end of data collection, the clinician integrates the information in a way that will inform and guide the course of treatment. A reliable and valid assessment strategy includes:[12]

- Multiple modes of measurement (e.g., observations, interviews, self-report scales)
- Multiple informants (i.e., parents, teachers, child, observers)
- Observation of behavior within multiple settings (i.e., home, school, community)
- Data collected at multiple time points.

Since most clinicians work under significant time and resource constraints, they must find ways to collect useful information from multiple sources at the lowest possible cost.

Each procedure used should yield unique information for constructing a treatment plan.[48] Given these parameters, a reasonable assessment strategy might include the following implementation methods:

1. Global rating scales completed by parents, children, and teachers
2. Clinical interviews with parents, children, and teachers
3. Observations of family interactions in the clinic and in the school or home
4. Repeated brief telephone interviews with parents
5. Examination of historical records

The clinician uses the information collected during each of these procedures to specify both positive and problem behaviors that the child currently displays. Further, the clinician identifies the strengths and problems present in the various environments in which the child interacts (i.e., home, school, and community). This information is then used to construct a tailored treatment plan (see chapter 3).

Implementing the Assessment Strategy

Handling the Initial Call

Objective — To infuse structure and improve the efficiency of the first face-to-face interview between the family and the clinician.

Process — The first call parents make to a treatment facility should lay the groundwork for the first face-to-face interview between the family and the clinician.[49] Clinic staff members that handle such calls can press for specific information, including the types and frequency of the child's problem behaviors, the dates of specific major problem incidents, and the general reaction of the parents to the problem. Parents can also be queried about previous treatment history as well as about how the child functions in major settings (i.e., home, school, and community). The staff member should also briefly describe the intake and treatment process and answer any questions.

At the end of the 10 to 15 minute call, the staff member should request that parents:

- Complete the behavior rating scales (mailed the same day as the call)

- Have the child (if age 10 years or older) complete appropriate behavioral rating scales

- Ask the child's school teacher(s) to complete a behavior rating scale

- Return all completed behavioral rating scales several days prior to the intake interview

Parents can be told that if forms are not returned prior to the day of the interview, their appointment will be postponed. Setting up this contingency screens out parents who are probably not ready to pursue treatment at the present time. A critical factor in treatment success is the parents' ability to promote consistent, structured activities. If parents cannot return questionnaires by a predetermined date, they probably will have even more difficulty fulfilling the requirements of a treatment program. On the other hand, a major portion of a clinician's case load may involve parents who have trouble with such requirements. These parents may be distrustful of authority and may not be willing to comply during the early phases of

This section presents a process for implementing an assessment strategy. This process involves:

Handling the Initial Call

Collecting Behavioral Rating Scales

Conducting the Intake Interview

Utilizing Other Assessment Measures

Presenting Assessment Results

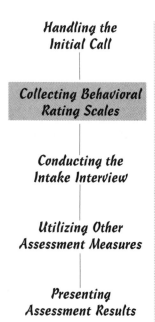

**Handling the
Initial Call**

**Collecting Behavioral
Rating Scales**

**Conducting the
Intake Interview**

**Utilizing Other
Assessment Measures**

**Presenting
Assessment Results**

The CBC-L norms may not be universally applicable, even within the U.S.[54,55]

***internal reliability**—the extent to which the various items on a test are related to one another*

***test-retest reliability**—the extent to which those tested obtain similar scores relative to each other on each administration of the test*

***inter-parental agreement**—the degree of agreement on test scores between parents*

***across-time correlations**—the extent to which a person's test scores remain in a similar rank compared to others across time. For example, if a test is highly stable, Suzy will tend to score high on three separate testings, Sam moderate, and Jean low.*

treatment. Thus, using such a screening approach might result in unjustly eliminating parents from a helpful treatment program that they might have completed.

Collecting Behavioral Rating Scales

Objective — To have parents, teachers, and the child estimate the type and severity of antisocial behaviors.

Process — Two useful questionnaires for diagnosing a conduct disorder are the Child Behavior Checklist (CBC-L) and the Disruptive Behavior Disorders Checklist (DBD).[50,51] Used together, these questionnaires yield estimates of both the type and severity of a child's antisocial behaviors.

- **CBC-L** — The CBC-L is widely used in both clinical and research settings. However, the CBC-L questions do not directly address all the DSM-IV conduct disorder behaviors. It comprises both a lengthy list of problem behaviors and numerous questions on academic and social functioning. It can be completed by parents, teachers, and youth (ages 11 to 18 years).[50,52,53] Scales of interest in terms of the conduct disorders (i.e., Delinquent Behavior, Aggressive Behavior, Attention Problems, and Anxious/Depressed) as well as prosocial functioning (e.g., Activities and Academic Performance) are computed by combining specific CBC-L items. Normative data allows the clinician to compare scores a child receives to those of a general population sample of children and adolescents.[54,55]

For the parent CBC-L, the following are moderate to strong for the conduct disorder-related scales:

- *Internal reliability*
- *Test-retest reliability*
- *Inter-parental agreement*
- *Across-time correlations*

Values for the youth CBC-L are similar, except for across-time correlations, which tend to be low.

The teacher CBC-L (called the Teacher Rating Form, or TRF) has similar psychometric properties, except that agreement between teachers tends to be moderate, especially on the Delinquent Behavior subscale.

In terms of validity, the CBC-L questionnaire items are *face-valid*. Further, both the parent and teacher conduct-disorder-related scales correlate moderately to strongly with similar scales from other self-report measures completed by parents or teachers. Finally, the parent, teacher, and youth CBC-L scores discriminate between clinic-referred and non-referred samples.[50,52,53]

- **DBD** — Although less psychometric information is available on the DBD, the items relate directly to the symptoms outlined in the DSM-IV for ADHD, CD and ODD. The DBD lists DSM-IV symptoms for ADHD, CD, and ODD, thereby facilitating total symptom counts for each disorder. In a large sample of boys in regular education classes as well as in a smaller sample of boys in special education classes, the internal reliabilities of the ADHD, CD, and ODD scales were strong.[51,56] Although empirical validity information is currently unavailable, the main advantage of the DBD is its clear face validity: the DBD items are the DSM-IV symptoms. Thus, having parents complete the scale is similar to asking them whether their child displays each of the symptoms of ADHD, CD, and ODD.

Scores on the DBD and/or the CBC-L can indicate that completion of further questionnaires might be useful. For example, if there are concerns about child depression, the Child Depression Inventory might be used to further assess child perceptions.[57] Thorough information about a variety of such "specialty" self-report scales are available from multiple sources listed in the Appendix.

Conducting the Intake Interview

Once the behavior rating forms have been returned, the clinician reviews the ratings as well as the background information and notes issues to pursue during the first intake meeting. Using these notes to guide content, the interview generally proceeds as follows:

1. The clinician greets the family and attempts to set a comfortable tone for the intake.

2. The clinician educates the family about the assessment process.

3. The clinician questions the parent(s) and child separately about the presenting problem and related issues.

4. The clinician arranges with the parents to collect further baseline assessment data.

face valid—*the content of test items directly assesses a self-evident psychological construct*

Many questionnaires have been developed that assess both child and family functioning.[58-60]

Handling the Initial Call

Collecting Behavioral Rating Scales

Conducting the Intake Interview

Utilizing Other Assessment Measures

Presenting Assessment Results

Parent Interview

Objective — In the parent interview, the clinician should:

1. Begin to establish a working alliance with the parents.

2. Gather specific information about the child's current problem behaviors and prosocial functioning.

3. Specify how problems are currently being dealt with by the parents, the school, and the community.

4. Gather the child's *developmental history* and a *psychosocial history.*

5. Query the parents regarding what they want to happen as a result of their contact with the clinician.

6. Make plans regarding follow up appointments.

developmental history— significant events and milestones during childhood such as age the child first walked, talked, etc.

psychosocial history— history of significant social developments such as family interactions, behavior in friendships, adjustment at school

Process — Prior to the interviews, the clinician integrates responses from the behavior rating scales (see pages 14-15, CBC-L, DBD) into a diagnostic framework by making a checklist that lists the possible diagnoses and their symptoms. This framework can be used to guide further questioning.

At the session beginning, the clinician should describe the intake process and inform the parents of the various intake and treatment details and time lines. Parents should be informed of any laws that dictate clinician behavior in certain situations, such as what the clinician must do if information is obtained about child abuse and neglect or a potential suicide or homicide. Prior to continuing, parents should be given a written informed consent form, which should be signed prior to moving forward with the interview.

Next, a brief history of the child and family should be taken as is relevant to the presenting problem. The history assists the clinician with diagnosis (e.g., Conduct Disorder, early onset subtype) as well as imparts a sense of how difficult the child's problems have been to deal with in the past. The clinician should query parents about:

Some parents may have difficulty with the suggested parent interview. Being flexible and varying the content, structure, and pacing of interventions is important throughout assessment and treatment, particularly with parents who have had negative experiences with previous mental health professionals or agencies.

- Onset of the presenting complaint or other behavior problems

- Development of symptoms across time

- Previous attempts to deal with the problem in professional and lay settings

- Family history of the problem

After clarifying the child's specific symptoms, the clinician can query the parents about their specific reactions to each problematic child behavior at home as well as the reactions of teachers and other adults in settings outside the home. This information provides the clinician with some knowledge of the rewards and punishments children receive for their antisocial behaviors.

The clinician should ask about the state of current family relationships, parental friendships, and parent-teacher relationships. Family participation in community and neighborhood life should also be queried. For example, knowing that a family closely identifies with or practices certain religious or cultural traditions is important information that can be incorporated into the intervention process as treatment progresses. During therapy, strengths present in each of these areas can help support changes in child behavior.

Parents should be asked what absolutely needs to be changed for them to feel that treatment is successful. This gives the clinician some idea about what the parent really wants from their visit to the clinic.

The parent intake interview ends with the clinician getting releases from the parents for all pertinent records (e.g., school records, juvenile court records) as well as permission to directly communicate with pertinent adults involved with the child (e.g., pediatrician, school personnel, previous clinicians). Arrangements are also made for other baseline assessments, such as multiple telephone calls with the Parent Daily Report (see telephone interview on page 20) and clinic, home, or school observations.

Child Interview

Objective — In the child intake interview, the clinician should:

1. Begin to establish a working alliance with the child

2. Learn about the child's perspective on the presenting problems

3. Gain knowledge about the child's friendship network and his relationships with significant adults

4. Determine the child's general intellectual and emotional functioning

In therapeutic interventions for the conduct disorders the clinician-child relationship is an important one, and a concerted effort needs to be made to develop a positive relationship.

The use of a brief mental status exam and/or neuropsychological screen is also quite helpful in deciding whether further testing is necessary.[58,59]

Process — To achieve the primary goal of establishing a working relationship with the child, the clinician should keep the tone of the interview light, questioning in a matter-of-fact manner that does not push or threaten the child. The actual interview questions often yield little new information. However, if children are willing to answer, their responses can be quite revealing about family functioning as well as peer relationships.

Besides informal questioning, a more formal structure can be imposed by administering several subscales from a standardized achievement test (e.g., the Woodcock-Johnson) and an intelligence test (e.g., the vocabulary section from the Wechsler Intelligence Scale for Children.[58,61] These measures provide the clinician with basic information on the child's current intellectual functioning and allow the clinician to observe the child under structured conditions. With this information, the clinician can decide whether or not to recommend further psychological testing.

Teacher Interview

Objective — During the teacher intake interview (usually done over the telephone), the clinician should:

1. Begin to establish a working alliance with the teacher (to facilitate possible school interventions during treatment)

2. Gather specific information about how the child's current problem behaviors impact academic and social functioning in the school setting

3. Learn how problem behaviors are currently being dealt with at school

4. Determine teacher perceptions about the relationship between the parents and the school.

Process — The clinician should query the teacher about each of the above areas. Specific questions should seek to clarify or expand the teacher's responses to the behavior rating scale.

Utilizing Other Assessment Methods

Following the intake interviews, the clinician should determine which standard assessment methods best fit the assessment strategy. These methods include:

• Standardized Clinical Interviews

Handling the Initial Call

Collecting Behavioral Rating Scales

Conducting the Intake Interview

Utilizing Other Assessment Measures

Presenting Assessment Results

- Common Psychometric Instruments (Rorschach Inkblot Test, MMPI-A, WISC-III)

- Telephone Interviews

- Observations

- Historical Records

At present there is no evidence that medical laboratory tests provide the clinician with information that would aid in diagnosing or treating any of the conduct disorders.

Standardized Clinical Interviews

Standardized diagnostic interviews may help clinicians diagnose conduct disorders more efficiently and reliably. One popular interview currently being adapted for the DSM-IV is the Diagnostic Interview for Children (DISC).[59,60] The DISC takes from 50 to 70 minutes for a trained person to administer and covers the major forms of child and adolescent psychopathology, including the mood, anxiety, disruptive-behavior, and substance-use disorders. Two versions of the DISC are available:

- DISC-C: for children ages six through 18

- DISC-P: for parents

With adolescents, test-retest reliabilities for the conduct disorder scales on the DISC-C are moderate to strong. However, with elementary school-aged children, the reliabilities of the DISC-C scales are quite low. In contrast, test-retest reliabilities for the DISC-P conduct-disorder scales are strong for children of all ages.[64] Agreement between parent and child on DISC diagnoses tends to be low.[65] In terms of validity, both DISC instruments discriminate between clinic-referred and non-referred samples.[66]

Common Psychometric Instruments (Rorschach Inkblot Test, MMPI-A, WISC-III)

For the conduct disorders, there is currently no evidence that frequently used psychometric instruments, such as the Rorschach Inkblot Test, the Minnesota Multiphasic Personality Inventory-Adolescent (MMPI-A), and the Weschler Intelligence Scale for Children-Third Edition (WISC-III), reveal information that leads to a more accurate conduct disorder diagnosis.[61,67,68]

The DISC was developed for use within highly supervised research situations. Versions of the test used by clinicians outside the realm of research projects have lower reliability values than those noted.[62,63]

These psychometric instruments are not ideal as part of standard assessment procedures for the conduct disorders because:

- *They take a significant amount of time to administer, score, and interpret.*

- *They ultimately yield information from only one informant (the child) using one assessment mode (self-report) within one setting (the clinic).*

If a preliminary assessment (or other information) leads the clinician to suspect the child of having a specific disability, and if there are no indications of a standardized assessment within the last few years, a reasonable next step is to pursue a new evaluation through the child's school.

However, administering portions of intelligence and achievement tests can be quite useful during the preliminary clinical interview with the child. Complete evaluations can be done in the clinic if parents request such a service. However, clinicians may want to investigate options available through the child's school. Free, school-sponsored evaluations of intelligence, achievement, speech and language, and motor development are mandated by Federal Law.[48] Obtaining such evaluations from the school may take some time, but in conduct disorder cases, the presenting problems (e.g., disobedience, aggression, stealing) are usually problematic enough that they need to be addressed prior to academic interventions anyway.

Telephone Interviews

The Parent Daily Report (PDR) is a brief behavioral checklist administered over the telephone for roughly five minutes by a trained staff member.[46,49] The PDR addresses child antisocial behaviors (including the symptoms of the conduct disorders) and can be customized to include parent-identified problem behaviors (i.e., all child behaviors identified by the parents as problematic at *baseline*). During the interview, parents report on the occurrence/non-occurrence of each behavior mentioned.

baseline—the period of time prior to the beginning of a therapeutic intervention

The PDR can be used to:

1. Establish the baseline level of child antisocial behavior (e.g., one to two weeks of daily PDR data can be collected to yield estimates of children's average performance as well as their day-to-day variability)

2. Monitor changes in antisocial behavior throughout treatment

It is best if the PDR is not administered by the treating clinician. This ensures data that is free from clinician bias.

PDR scores collected during treatment (typically one to five calls per week) can be plotted and compared to the data collected during baseline to visually track how a child's antisocial behaviors change during the course of treatment.

Repeated measures of data collected with the PDR allows clinicians to conduct much more powerful studies of treatment outcome than simply using pre-post global self-report measures such as the CBC-L.[70,71]

Based on several studies, the PDR appears to be a reliable and valid measure of problem behavior.[72] Inter-interviewer reliability for the PDR is generally quite high.[69] Test-retest reliability for scores from one day to the next is moderate. However, data summarized from several PDRs (i.e., the average of several scores) is more reliable. In terms of validity, total scores for targeted problem behaviors on the PDR correlate significantly with both home observational data and global self-reports of the same behaviors.[69]

Observations

Through observation, the clinician can assess the frequency, intensity, and quality of a child's antisocial and prosocial behaviors on a moment-by-moment basis. Responses of parents, siblings, peers, and teachers can also be assessed, giving the clinician clues about the types of rewards and punishments children receive for the negative and positive behaviors they display. If observations are done in the home or at school, the clinician can also assess the broader social and physical characteristics of the environments in which children spend most of their time.[73]

Live or videotaped observation of the child's behavior provides the clinician with a wealth of information.

Structuring Observations — The most common observation tasks are:

1. **A play task for use with younger children and their parents.** The child and a parent play together with the toys and games of their choice, clean-up, and then participate in several structured, goal-directed activities (e.g., parent directs child in a parent-chosen activity, completing a maze, child teaches parent a game, working on an art project together).[74]

2. **A problem-solving task for use with older children and adolescents.** During this task, the child and parents attempt to discuss and generate solutions to a current family problem.[75]

The advantages of tasks one and two are that they can be done in the clinic in 10 to 15 minutes, they can be easily videotaped for later viewing by the clinician and the parents, and they present families with a standard "testing" situation.

3. **Unstructured home observations.** An independent rater or the clinician observes the child and family in their home during the dinner hour or early evening.[76]

4. **Live observations of the child in the classroom and on the playground.**[73,74]

The advantage of tasks three and four are that they take place in the child's natural environments. However, such tasks require more staff time to complete.

Coding Observations — To code family interactions, independent observers or clinicians can use a simple behavioral coding system. The Parent-Child Interaction Coding System (PCIS) and Family Observation Schedule (FOS) are relatively easy to learn and use.[48,73] Both systems include codes for parent commands, parent negative statements, child compliance, and child noncompliance. Since these behaviors are often at the center of conflict in families with a child diagnosed with a conduct disorder, the PCIS and FOS are ideal for capturing

When coders receive training and consistent monitoring, evidence supports the reliability and validity of these coding systems. Unfortunately, the reliability and validity of the systems in the general clinical context are unknown.

clinically relevant information as well as for monitoring changes during treatment.

To code the behavior of a child during school, again, a simple coding system should be employed. One possible system is the Direct Observation Form (DOF) comprising similar items to the aforementioned parent and teacher CBC-L forms.[76] To code the DOF, the independent observer or clinician watches the child in a school setting for a 10-minute period (e.g., classroom, recess, lunch time) and then completes and scores the form. Subscales on the DOF that are of particular relevance to the conduct disorders include Aggressive Behavior, On Task, Hyperactive, Attention Demanding, and Depressed. The clinician should repeat the 10-minute observation procedure within the same setting on different days several times (e.g., a total of four times in the classroom), and take an average of the DOF scores for the child's final score. Several randomly-selected children (or several children identified by the teacher as "average") in the class can also be observed and rated, giving the clinician information on how the child compares to his or her classmates. The DOF has good *interobserver reliability* and *correlates* with other measures of behavioral problems.[76,78] Further, scores on the DOF discriminate between referred and non-referred samples.[78]

Besides the use of formal coding systems during observations, clinicians or observers should write narrative descriptions or complete questionnaires that document their general impressions of the child and his or her surroundings.[79] Several observer impression questionnaires have been developed to index a variety of child prosocial and antisocial behaviors as well as parenting behaviors and styles. These questionnaires tend to have good reliability and to correlate moderately with other measures of conduct disorder and parenting behaviors.[79,80]

Historical Records

If parents consent, official records afford a low-cost, potentially high-yield assessment opportunity.[81] Treatment records will provide the clinician with session notes kept during treatment, behavioral observations recorded during inpatient or residential stays, and/or testing data from previous psychological assessments. Academic records document standardized testing, grades, discipline contacts, and developmental problems. Medical records may document parental complaints or

---

Although there are numerous reliable coding systems available, (some of which also have validity data) many are difficult to use outside a research group setting.[74,77]

inter-observer reliability— degree of agreement among the ratings of various observers

correlates—the extent to which two scores are linearly related to each other (e.g., as one score goes up, the other tends to go up or down)

include comments about the child's behavior over time, providing a different point of view on the child's developmental history. Juvenile court records document formal police contacts with the child (e.g., detainment for suspected criminal activity). Child protective services division contacts due to reported child abuse or neglect may be incorporated into juvenile court records as well as documented in separate agency records. However, information gained from historical records should be interpreted with caution, for it may be quite incomplete and/or inaccurate. For example, less than five percent of juvenile-reported crimes result in police arrest and official documentation.[82]

Presenting Assessment Results

Once baseline assessment has been completed, the clinician integrates the collected information in a manner that will facilitate treatment planning and treatment process. Based on the current knowledge of the development of the conduct disorders, simply tallying up whether or not to diagnose a conduct disorder is not very helpful for treatment planning. Such a tally will undoubtedly reveal that the various people that were queried do not agree on the nature and/or extent of the problem. It may even reveal that they do not agree on whether or not a problem exists. For example, in several studies where parents, teachers, and/or children were asked about the child's antisocial behavior, 55 to 95 percent of the children given a conduct disorder diagnosis were identified by only one respondent.[6,83]

Some raters tend to rate a child as having conduct problems more than others. Elementary school teachers are three times more likely to identify a child as displaying a conduct disorder than are parents, and adolescents are two to three times more likely to identify themselves as meeting diagnostic criteria than their parents.[6] This high rate of reporting by adolescents has been found in several large surveys, with greater than 50 percent of adolescents admitting to committing more than one kind of antisocial behavior.[84,85]

A more practical and useful way to integrate information is through the use of a descriptive analysis framework.[73,86] During a descriptive analysis, the clinician considers how specific problem behaviors might be related to what happens in the surrounding environment. The clinician uses the complete set

*Handling the
Initial Call*

*Collecting Behavioral
Rating Scales*

*Conducting the
Intake Interview*

*Utilizing Other
Assessment Measures*

*Presenting
Assessment Results*

A descriptive analysis specifies:

1. Antecedents
   a. External
   b. Internal

2. Behavior

3. Consequences

of data to specify the following for each problem behavior (e.g., hitting a sibling):

1. **Antecedents** —

   a. **External:** conditions that exist external to the child prior to the occurrence of a problem behavior (e.g., child and sibling are playing together)

   b. **Internal:** conditions that exist within the child that may be related to the problem behavior (e.g., hitting is more likely when a child is tired after a long day at school and daycare)

2. **Behavior** — the problem behavior itself (e.g., hitting a sibling)

3. **Consequences** — conditions that exist immediately after the problem behaviors occur (e.g., parent yells at child to stop hitting and return toy to sibling, child yells back at parent, parent and child argue, parent backs off).

See chapter 3 for more discussion on the development of the conduct disorders.

The clinician then hypothesizes about how the antecedents, problem behavior, and consequences relate to each other (e.g., repeated occurrences of such situations that teach children to use aversive behavior to get what they want). Such hypotheses are then used to guide and focus the treatment plan. Decisions can be made about what is appropriate for the clinician to deal with during treatment, and what issues should be immediately referred elsewhere (e.g., individual therapy for parents, marital therapy, psychiatric consult for possible medication assessment).

See chapter 3 for detailed descriptions of treatment interventions.

Once the clinician compiles the relevant information and makes tentative plans for treatment, decisions must be made on how best to present this information to the family. The cornerstone of successful treatment is for parents and clinician to arrive at a common perception of the problem and potential solutions.[72]

Assessment results are usually presented to the parents and the child during separate meetings. "Guided Participation" is a useful framework for such a presentation.[73] The clinician alternates summarizing the results and implications of the assessment with time for parents to think about, discuss, and question the clinician's reasoning. After presenting the data and listening to parental feedback, the clinician introduces the treatment model that seems most appropriate for the child's problem, specifies the goals for the proposed intervention, discusses how long the intervention will likely last, and explains how much treatment will cost the family.

What Other Disorders Commonly Occur with Conduct Disorders?

According to DSM-IV, CD can be diagnosed if the specified criteria are met, whether or not other psychiatric diagnoses exist.[5] However, a diagnosis of ODD is given only if the symptoms occur independently of a Mood or Psychotic Disorder and if the symptoms are distinguishable from those of ADHD. For example, children displaying attention-deficit-disordered symptoms such as inattention, impulsivity, and hyperactivity often exhibit associated symptoms of ODD such as noncompliance. To diagnose co-occurring ODD and ADHD, the clinician must decide that in addition to ADHD symptoms, the child is truly exhibiting hostile, angry, and defiant behavior.

Several or all of the key symptoms of an Attention Deficit Disorder (inattention, impulsivity, and hyperactivity) may occur for a variety of reasons besides the presence of ADHD. For example, children who have experienced trauma, such as abuse, may display several ADHD-like symptoms.

Co-occurring Disorders

The conduct disorders frequently co-occur with other types of child psychopathology. As a result, the clinician needs to probe a wide range of symptomatology during the assessment phase of treatment.

In a study that combined data from several major population studies, 13 percent of children received a diagnosis of CD or ODD. Of that 13 percent:

During adolescence in particular, substance use disorders are likely to co-occur with the conduct disorders.[87]

- Twenty-one percent were also diagnosed with a mood disorder such as Major Depression or Bipolar.

- Twenty-four percent were also diagnosed with an anxiety disorder.

- Thirty-one percent were also diagnosed with an attention deficit disorder.[88]

In samples of children diagnosed with an attention deficit disorder, as many as 65 percent may display significant levels of defiance.[89] Across a variety of studies, up to 40 percent of children diagnosed with ADHD and 65 percent of adolescents diagnosed with ADHD meet full diagnostic criteria for ODD, and 20 to 50 percent of these children and adolescents also meet full diagnostic criteria for CD.[48] The co-occurrence of ADHD and the conduct disorders is high enough that there is some debate about whether they are actually distinct behavioral syndromes, or rather parts of the same syndrome.[90]

**Therapy Notes
from the Desk of
Pat Owen**

Mother reported that Shawn was picked up by police for shoplifting this week. Shawn had contact with the police in the past, and now has been put on probation. Further therapy sessions are part of the conditions of the probation. Assessments completed from parents and teachers. Teachers report that Shawn has grown increasingly defiant and argumentative. From parent report, Shawn does have a significant amount of time each day when he is unsupervised. Will develop a behavior program that links behavior at home and at school. This would likely stabilize and improve Shawn's day-to-day life. Recommend that stepfather begin to attend sessions and find ways to be more involved in the parenting and family activities.

Chapter Three: Treating the Conduct Disorders

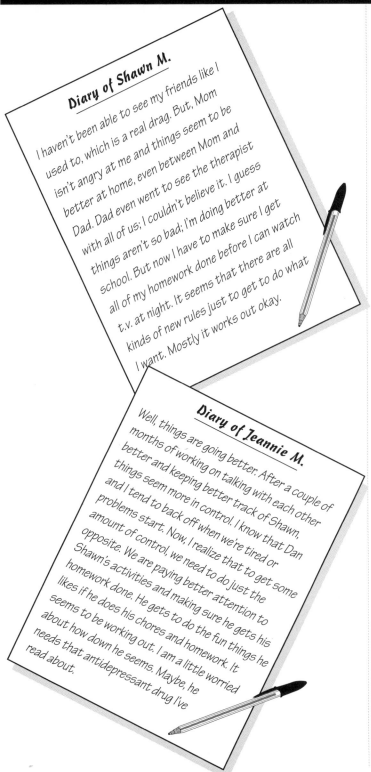

Diary of Shawn M.

I haven't been able to see my friends like I used to, which is a real drag. But, Mom isn't angry at me and things seem to be better at home, even between Mom and Dad. Dad even went to see the therapist with all of us; I couldn't believe it. I guess things aren't so bad; I'm doing better at school. But now I have to make sure I get all of my homework done before I can watch t.v. at night. It seems that there are all kinds of new rules just to get to do what I want. Mostly it works out okay.

Diary of Jeannie M.

Well, things are going better. After a couple of months of working on talking with each other and keeping better track of Shawn, things seem more in control. I know that Dan and I tend to back off when we're tired or problems start. Now, I realize that to get some opposite. We are paying better attention to Shawn's activities and making sure he gets his homework done. He gets to do the fun things he likes if he does his chores and homework. It seems to be working out. I am a little worried about how down he seems. Maybe, he needs that antidepressant drug I've read about.

This chapter answers the following:

- **What are the Environmentally Based Approaches to Treating the Conduct Disorders?**—This section presents environmentally based etiology and treatment methodology for behavior therapy, cognitive therapy, family therapy, group therapy, and the psychodynamic approach.

- **What are the Biological Influences and Treatments for the Conduct Disorders?**—This section focuses on the use and efficacy of using medications as adjuncts to psyhotherapy.

Issues to consider when treating children and adolescents diagnosed with a conduct disorder are:

1. Basis of the Diagnosis

2. Focus of the Treatment Program

3. Scientific Support for the Use of Psychological Treatment

4. Use of Medications as a Secondary Treatment

Basis of the Diagnosis—Conduct disorders are diagnosed solely on the basis of child behaviors. The most effective treatment programs focus on changing specific problematic behaviors.

Focus of the Treatment Program—Conduct problems are developed and maintained through a child's social interactions with parents, teachers, and peers. The most effective treatment programs focus first on changing the characteristics of these interactions.

Scientific Support for the Use of a Psychological Treatment—Research studies, such as randomized clinical trials, support the use of some treatment programs, most notably Parent Training and certain school- and community-based behavior management and problem-solving skills programs. The most effective treatment programs use Parent Training in combination with one or more of the other programs.

Use of Medications as a Secondary Treatment—For some children, medications may decrease the intensity or frequency of certain conduct-disordered behaviors, which in turn may improve the child's response to ongoing psychosocial interventions.[95] Typically, physicians prescribe medications when:

- The conduct disorder co-occurs with an Attention Deficit Hyperactivity Disorder (ADHD).

- The conduct disorder includes displays of severe and extreme aggression, destruction, and violence.

The most effective treatment programs use medication, if indicated, as an adjunct to psychological therapy, rather than as the sole treatment method.

Over 250 different types of psychological therapies are practiced with children and adolescents.[91] Rather than being grounded in basic scientific research, most of these therapies are buttressed by large bodies of theoretical and anecdotal literature.[92]

Of these therapies, Parent Training has emerged as the clear treatment of choice for children and adolescents exhibiting conduct-disordered behavior.[93,94]

What are the Environmentally Based Approaches to Treating the Conduct Disorders?

In this section, we review the most common approaches to treating the conduct disorders. These approaches are:

- *Behavior Therapy*—Behavior Therapy attempts to change the social interactions between parents, teachers, peers, and the child that may promote negative behavior. Theorists hypothesize that such interactions inadvertently teach and reinforce a child to repeat verbal and physical aggression as well as other conduct problems.

- *Cognitive Therapy*—Cognitive Therapy attempts to change the thought processes, or cognitions, of a child diagnosed with conduct disorder. Theorists hypothesize that certain cognitions lead to child aggressive behaviors and interpersonal conflict, while others may be conducive to positive social interactions.

- *Family Therapy*—Family Therapy attempts to change family communication processes. Proponents believe that problematic interactions between family members create and maintain child conduct problems.

- *Group Therapy*—Group Therapy attempts to change various aspects of the social networks children have with their peers. Proponents hypothesize that unsupervised contact with antisocial peers plays a key role in the escalation and maintenance of child conduct problems. Similarly, adult supervised contact with peers without behavior problems leads to more positive child behaviors.

- *Psychodynamic Therapy*—Psychodynamic Therapy attempts to change parent-child interactions. Theorists believe that children who experienced poor caregiving during early childhood may have difficulty developing and maintaining positive social relationships. Additionally, those children are thought to be particularly vulnerable to exhibiting conduct-disordered behaviors.

The following sections present each therapy type in terms of basic parameters, content and process of treatment sessions, follow-up methods after termination, and research findings on treatment efficacy.

The primary goal of treatment is to change the child's environment so that it will strengthen the child's prosocial behavioral repertoire.

The primary goal of treatment is to provide children with a cognitive framework that will help them better solve interpersonal problems.

What is the Behavioral Therapy Approach to Treating the Conduct Disorders?

There are several different versions of behavior therapy. This section focuses on a version called Social Learning Theory.[96,97]

Behavioral theorists hypothesize that the social interactions between a child with conduct disorder and his or her parents, teachers, and peers inadvertently teach and maintain aggressive and other antisocial child behaviors. Theorists label this process "basic training," and hypothesize that it occurs through the unintended *negative reinforcement* of aversive behaviors.

For example, consider the following sequence of events:

negative reinforcement—the discontinuation of an undesired event (e.g., parents fighting) following a behavior (e.g. child hits sibling) rewards the occurrence of that behavior (i.e. the hit)

Interaction sequences such as these are called "coercive interactions."

1. A parent tells a child to put a candy bar back on the shelf at the grocery store checkout line.

2. The child complains and whines.

3. The parent repeats the request more sternly.

4. The child says "no."

5. The parent threatens to punish the child.

6. The child yells.

7. The parent threatens, and the child yells louder.

The sequence ends when the parent backs down; the child stops yelling; and the parent purchases the candy bar. Unfortunately, the discontinuation of the parent's threat increases the likelihood that the child will yell again when in a similar demand situation. Further, the discontinuation of the child's yelling increases the likelihood that the parent will back down again in a similar situation.

positive reinforcement—the delivery of a desired event (e.g., parent says, "Great job, Joe!" and gives Joe a hug) following a behavior (e.g., child playing nicely with sibling) which results in an increase of that behavior

When negative reinforcement sequences occur again and again within a relationship, the participants are "taught" that aversive behaviors are effective at "shutting off" the negativity of others. Unfortunately, when such behavior sequences predominate in a family, *positive reinforcement* sequences are usually quite scarce. Over time, one result of a high rate of negative reinforcement and a low rate of positive reinforcement within a family is a child who is deficient in positive social skills and extremely proficient in deviant behaviors. Another result is the withdrawal of parents from parent-child interaction, which provides the child with more adult-unsupervised time both inside and outside the home.

Children who are skilled in deviant behaviors and who have low levels of adult supervision tend to have difficulties in conventional situations, such as school and on the playground. A common outcome of conflict in these situations is rejection by peers and adults. In concert, difficulties in school and with peers can lead to a cascading set of problems for the child, the family, and the community.[12,97] If a child then begins to associate with peers involved in delinquent activities (i.e., deviant peers), the child will likely be exposed to and begin to participate in more serious antisocial behaviors (e.g., violent acts), as well as other problem behaviors, such as early sexual behavior and substance use.

Coercive family processes provide both the means and the opportunity for a child to learn and practice aversive behaviors across multiple settings, behaviors that ultimately lead to the diagnosis of Conduct Disorder.

There are three recommended primary behavioral treatment programs for the Conduct Disorders and they are:

- Parent Training
- School-Based Programs (CLASS and RECESS)
- Multidimensional Treatment Foster Care

Parent Training

Ample evidence exists that parent behaviors such as inconsistent discipline and inadequate supervision are related to child conduct problems.[12,97] On the basis of these findings, clinicians have designed Parent Training interventions to help redirect parents' efforts from inadvertently shaping problem behaviors to systematically teaching prosocial behaviors. Parent Training helps parents become effective "behavior modifiers" who accurately monitor what problems exist within their family, make plans to resolve such problems, and implement these plans.

Although many versions of Parent Training exist for treating the conduct disorders, one of the earliest and most influential programs was developed by Gerald R. Patterson and John B. Reid and their colleagues at the Oregon Social Learning Center (OSLC).[49,98] This program has been adapted to a variety of treatment settings and embodies many of the primary elements of current Parent Training programs.[12,97]

A variety of group and individual Parent Training treatment programs are available. See the Appendix: Recommended Resources for a list of these programs.

Basic Parameters. Parents attend treatment sessions, typically held weekly for 60 to 90 minutes. The child diagnosed with a conduct disorder also attends many sessions, and siblings are asked to come to family problem solving and negotiation sessions during the later part of treatment.

This treatment program was designed for children in elementary school or for those in early-to-mid adolescence. Content adaptations can be made for older or younger children.

Clinicians supplement sessions with frequent telephone calls (i.e., one to two per week). Frequent phone calls are particularly common during the initial stages of treatment. During the calls, the clinician and the parent troubleshoots the behavioral programs parents use with their children. A staff member other than the clinician makes separate calls to collect Parent Daily Report (PDR) data for monitoring treatment effectiveness. (For more information on using the PDR in telephone interviews, see page 20.)

The average length of treatment is three to four months; however, termination should be a joint decision between clinician and family.[48] Average clinician contact time during treatment is 20 to 40 hours, approximately one-third of which is spent on the telephone.[95]

Parent Training involves an assessment and a treatment phase.

Assessment Phase—The clinician attempts to build a well-defined and positive working relationship with the parents. For this relationship to be effective, the clinician should:

1. **Build a trusting relationship with the parents**. Make frequent phone contacts and home visits, to gather the information needed to remove potential barriers. Spend time listening to parents, validating their feelings, and empathizing with their situation.

2. **Treat the parents as expert colleagues**. Instruct, advise, and support parents in a respectful fashion. Build on the strengths of a family.

3. **Actively model the techniques that are being taught**. Illustrate the use of appropriate skills at every opportunity. Invite all family members to selected family problem-solving sessions, and show parents how to appropriately involve children in family decisions.

Another important assessment phase goal is to teach parents to more accurately observe their own and their child's behavior. This process begins in earnest during the PDR phone calls that occur in the two-week baseline period following the face-to-face intake meeting. During these calls, clinicians guide parents to focus on observable child behaviors and succinctly report on what they observe.

Following the initial, two-week baseline assessment, the clinician asks parents to read a book on the principles of social learning theory and treatment (see the Appendix: Recommended

Depending on the needs of a particular family, parents also learn to:[49,73,100]

1. Communicate and work together more effectively with teachers and school administrators

2. Tutor their child in academic skills

3. Work out marital problems that interfere with parenting

4. Deal with other personal issues that can interfere with parenting, such as feelings of depression[101]

During this phase, observations in the home or clinician's office provides direct information about family functioning. Directly observing family processes stresses the importance of what family members do with each other on a moment-by-moment basis.

Resources). Once parents have read this material, the clinician tests the parents on their newly learned knowledge.

The process of a making a baseline assessment, asking parents to read, and testing knowledge prior to treatment screens those families where:

1. Either one or both parents are not ready to enter treatment.
2. The parents do not want to pursue a Parent Training-type of therapy.
3. The parents need more time to think about what they really want to do about their current situation.

During the next visit, the clinician presents and discusses baseline PDR information and the results of the book test, and highlights family and child concerns and strengths.

After this presentation, if the parents remain interested in continuing treatment, the child joins the parents, and the clinician teaches the family observational skills by having them track and record simple, well-defined behaviors during the session.

For example, the clinician asks family members to observe how many times the clinician blinks during a five-minute period. The clinician then takes all the data collected and calculates *rate-per-minute* summaries (e.g., 10 blinks in five-minutes is equivalent to a rate of two behaviors per minute).

Often, various family members' ratings do not match. This provides the opportunity for the clinician to discuss how difficult it is to accurately track even simple behaviors and then to present ideas for improving parental tracking. The clinician then helps parents pinpoint two problematic and two desired child behaviors and asks the parents to track these four behaviors over the next three days for two, pre-specified hours each day (i.e., each parent tracks for one hour).

After training the parents in the presence of the child, the clinician engages the child in the discussion, and fully explains what will be happening at home and why. The clinician asks the child to develop a list of desired changes for the family and to bring the list back to the next session.

At the end of the session, the clinician asks the parents to pay a "breakage fee" (with the actual amount adjusted for family income). Although this fee can be used to cover the cost of materials (e.g., the social learning book), it functions primarily as a

During Parent Training, clinicians teach parents to:

1. *Track and record specific behaviors*
2. *Setup, maintain, and modify a "contingency contract"*
3. *Deliver effective positive reinforcements to family members*
4. *Correctly utilize "Time Outs" as a consequence for child misbehavior*
5. *Control their anger during frustrating and conflicting parent-child interactions*
6. *Effectively monitor a child's whereabouts and behaviors*
7. *Use family conferences to solve and to prevent problems*

rate-per-minute—*the average number of specific behaviors of interest occurring in one minute*

Because many antisocial behaviors occur infrequently, a rate-per-day or a rate-per-week summary may be more appropriate.

The full "breakage fee" amount is refunded if parents meet all treatment program expectations.

penalty fund. For example, if parents arrive late or miss scheduled appointments, money can be deducted from the fund. Additional fees can be collected if the fund becomes exhausted.

On each of the next three days following this appointment, the clinician calls the parents at a prearranged time. During these calls, the clinician asks for the rate per minute of the four target behaviors and the length of time each parent observed the target behaviors. If the original behavioral definitions have proven to be difficult to use, the clinician helps refine them. Each call generally lasts no longer than five minutes per parent. During the third call, the clinician schedules the first Treatment Phase appointment.

With more serious or difficult cases (and/or with adolescents) it may be best to have a therapist work separately with the child during the early stages of treatment. Alternatively, clinicians may prefer to teach parents basic skills prior to the child joining treatment sessions.

Treatment Phase—The three main tasks for the clinician are:

1. Teaching the family new skills

2. Assisting the family in applying these skills to their specific situation

3. Creating and maintaining a regular family conference

The PDR calls continue throughout the entire treatment phase.

contingency contracting— a plan for the positive and negative consequences that follow specific child behaviors

During the first sessions, the clinician teaches the basic parenting skills of positive reinforcement, *contingency contracting*, and time out using the methods of discussion, modeling, and role-playing. For example, positive reinforcement skills include:

- Establishing eye contact

- Labeling the behavior being supported

- Using an enthusiastic tone of voice (e.g., looking at the child, the parent says "John, I really appreciate that you took out the trash. Thanks so much!")

"Yes, but…" statements are cloaked as reinforcers, but are really punishing statements.

The clinician helps parents deliver unqualified reinforcers (e.g., "Yes, you did a good job!"), rather than the all-too-common "Yes, but…" statements. For parents who have trouble expressing warmth, the clinician can work intensely with the parent on various ways to express positive emotion.

Parents learn a variety of techniques to increase the chances that their child will display positive behaviors. These techniques include:

1. Modeling the desired positive behaviors

2. Actively using positive reinforcement skills with all the children in the family, particularly during times when siblings are being cooperative with each other

3. Practicing ways to clearly describe to the child those behaviors desired by the parents as well as the positive consequences they will receive for such behaviors

The content and process of parent training must be adapted to the needs, problems, and strengths of each family.

Contingency Contracts—To facilitate the use of positive reinforcement, parents are taught to write and use a contingency contract. A contingency contract is a written document agreed upon by family members that specifies desired and undesired behaviors and details the positive or negative consequences for the display of such behaviors. The contract outlines a simple *token economy system* in which children earn points for displaying specific behaviors. Earned points can be exchanged for rewards from a pre-selected menu (e.g., playing a game with a parent or watching a favorite TV show).

token economy system—a program of earning points or other currency that can be traded in for specific rewards

The first contract parents use focuses solely on a few positive behaviors (e.g., doing what is asked, playing nicely with siblings). Parents give rewards frequently as the child displays these positive behaviors. Once this type of contract works well at home, parents develop a new contract using the PDR data that has been collected since the parent first began the Assessment Phase. The new contract:

1. Specifies one desired behavior (e.g., doing chores) and one undesired behavior (e.g., noncompliance).

2. Lists how many points can be earned or lost whenever the child displays each of these behaviors.

3. Lists rewards for earning a specific number of positive points as well as consequences for having zero or negative points at the end of the day (e.g., going to bed 30 minutes early).

More advanced contracts include more behaviors.

Time Out—Once parents are proficient in positive reinforcement and contingency contracting, the clinician introduces nonviolent discipline techniques, such as Time Out. Time Out is an alternative punishment to yelling, spanking, or grounding. Clinicians model for and role-play with parents how to give effective Time Outs. Parents are taught to give a child one warning following the occurrence of the problem behavior. If the behavior continues, parents are instructed to tell their child to go to a predetermined, out of the way place

For older children, substitute work consequences for Time Out.

Time outs should be given in a room that is free from the distractions created by other family members and that is perceived as boring by the child (e.g., the bathroom).

Parents are instructed not to physically take their child to Time Out, and not to engage their child in a discussion or argument during Time Out.

Because Parent Training techniques serve to reduce the intensity and modify the quality of discipline confrontations, effective Parent Training should ultimately reduce parent distress and anger.

As the child's behavior gets under control, the number of Time Outs parents need to give should drop. If this does not occur within seven to 14 days, parents are likely misusing the techniques.

that the child perceives as boring (e.g., the bathroom). Time Outs are brief, and usually begin at 3 to 5 minutes in length. If the child refuses to go, their time in Time Out is slowly increased in one minute increments until they do go. If the Time Out reaches a predetermined maximum such as 10 minutes, parents withdraw a privilege for a small period of time (e.g., watching television for the rest of the afternoon). Parents are warned that introducing Time Out on a consistent basis into a family is often quite challenging, and that the clinician will try to assist during this difficult adjustment period by calling and consulting with the parents on a daily basis. Finally, the clinician explains Time Out to the child and engages the child in role-playing to demonstrate how this technique works.

Clinicians may find it helpful to review simple anger control techniques with the parents. Sometimes, teaching parents how to accurately recognize when they are becoming angry can help circumvent problems. Encouraging parents to give themselves five-minute Time Outs or to count to 10 prior to speaking to their child can diffuse volatile situations. In extreme circumstances, parents may be asked to sign a contract specifying that instead of expressing their anger verbally or physically against family members, they will call the clinician the first moment they are beginning to feel angry. For some parents, this type of contract can help disrupt angry outbursts and can assist the parent in beginning to use more constructive communication techniques.

The clinician informs parents that correct, consistent use of the contingency contract and of Time Outs typically results in predetermined, target problem behaviors coming under some parental control in seven to 14 days.

In between treatment sessions, the clinician continues to call the parents once or twice a week so that issues are dealt with immediately that could disrupt the positive teaching relationship established between the parents and the child. As noted earlier, the clinician or another staff member also continues to make separate data-collection PDR calls to monitor child behavior changes.

Structured Weekly Sessions—Once parents begin to use contingency contracting and Time Out in the home, the clinician can use these five techniques in the following week's session to refine the family's basic skills:

1. Detail what happened at home with the contract during the previous week, and provide the family ample praise for positive results and efforts.

2. Review PDR data.

3. Review data collected by the parents on any new problem behaviors they would like to address.

Ask parents to collect data on new problem behaviors they would like to change.

4. Expand the contract by specifying new behaviors and/or changing rewards and/or delaying rewards.

5. Spend the last 10 to 15 minutes of the sessions dealing with family crises or other topics, as necessary.

During these weekly sessions, one of the primary teaching formats used is the role-playing of reinforcement and discipline scenarios. Parents practice together or with the clinician, and the clinician then provides feedback on their performance. One particularly useful role-playing technique is the "wrong way–right way" method.[85] Parents are instructed to role-play a parent-child interaction the wrong way, and the clinician praises their "good" acting abilities. This gives the clinician the opportunity to comment on ineffective or problematic parenting in a nonthreatening and disengaged context. It also allows parents to discuss and acknowledge how miserable it feels to be a parent in a "wrong way" situation.

Next, the clinician instructs the parent how to act the "right way." The clinician actively, but gently, shapes the role-play as necessary. This can be done by whispering in the ear of one or both participants. This technique can be particularly useful when parents act out difficult interactions they experienced with their child during the previous week.

After parents master these basic skills, the clinician presents more advanced parenting skills, such as monitoring and family problem solving.

Monitoring—As children reach adolescence, monitoring youth activities when they are away from home is crucial to limiting the extent and growth of conduct problems. Youth who spend unsupervised time with deviant friends are particularly likely to commit antisocial acts.[13,37] During treatment, the clinician teaches parents to be specific about their adolescents' whereabouts and schedules throughout the day. Parents learn to ensure compliance with the planned schedule. Behaviors related to staying on schedule are written into the contingency contract and appropriate consequences are detailed.

Clinicians need to encourage parents to get to know and to keep in regular contact with their child's friends and the friends' parents.

37

A fundamental message of Parent Training is that all family members have an equal stake in the functioning of the family.

Basic Family Conference Structure:

1. Discussing the pleasant high points for the family during the week

2. Reviewing problems that arose during the week

3. Conducting problem solving, if necessary (e.g., pinpointing the problem, brainstorming possible solutions, choosing the best solution)

4. Documenting the problem-solving results

5. Planning a family activity that promotes family prosocial interaction.

Children participate as equal partners with parents in family conferences that dominate the later phase of Parent Training. Thus, the entire family receives direct instruction on how to solve family problems.

Family Conferences—During the final stage of treatment, siblings join the parents and child in treatment sessions. Family members learn how to plan and conduct family conferences and to construct, modify, and change contracts to help solve family problems.

During treatment sessions, the clinician helps families follow the conference structure appropriately. At first, parents lead the conference; later, the child and siblings take turns leading. Family members take turns documenting decisions made during the meeting. Members also make formal contracts specifying what is to happen as a result of the decisions and when the contract will be renegotiated.

Families generate a set of rules to govern the way family members communicate with each other during conferences. For example:

1. Each person's opinion is of equal worth during a conference.

2. The person who perceives themselves as the "victim" in a particular situation is always right. Family members are encouraged to help the victim pinpoint the problem, and members paraphrase the problem. The "victim" provides feedback about the accuracy of their paraphrasing.

Frequently, clinicians videotape the structured family conferences. When reviewing the tape, the clinician can discuss ways for the family to improve the process of the family conference. For family members who are having trouble accepting that positive changes are actually happening, videotaping can also highlight the positive behaviors of certain family members (e.g., the positive behaviors of the child).

As the family improves their ability to conduct family conferences, the clinician should expand the purpose of family meetings to deal with the family crises that likely arose during the previous week. The clinician encourages families to conduct and to tape record additional weekly conferences at home. These recordings help the clinician provide targeted feedback of family progress and monitor the generalization of skills to the home setting.

Intensive Interventions—At least 20 percent of parents respond poorly to clinic visits and phone calls, and require more intensive intervention.[49] For these parents, home visits can be conducted during which the clinician assesses family interaction, role plays appropriate behaviors, and supervises the correct performance of skills. Home visits should be used if clear changes in child behavior are not observed within three weeks after contingency contracting begins. During a home visit, the clinician can point out problems as they naturally occur and follow this up with immediate role-playing and modeling of what can be done to improve parent effectiveness.

One or two such visits may be sufficient for some families, but more intensive work in the home may be required for others.[49]

Follow-up After Program Termination—Families are encouraged to call for "booster shot" meetings with the clinician as needed. Approximately 50 percent of families request such a service. In one study, 12 of 28 families requested additional intervention for an average of seven hours during the first year after treatment termination. The average decreased to four hours during the second year and one hour during the third year.[99]

Good Parent Training is "Family Training."

What is the Effectiveness of Parent Training Programs?

The impact of Parent Training on child antisocial behavior has been studied extensively, and the research literature has been reviewed myriad times.[21,98,102] Most researchers have focused on immediate or short-term outcomes, and many have found positive treatment effects. With the OSLC program, approximately one in three families benefits from the standard techniques of Parent Training. With more extensive outpatient interventions (such as school interventions), the initial success rate can probably approach two out of three families.[49] The Parent Training program that has been most rigorously investigated is that of Carolyn Webster-Stratton. This video-based program has been found to be an effective intervention program for children with conduct problems within a variety of different samples.[103-106] Factors that appear to improve treatment success include:

1. Offering parents as many sessions as needed

2. Using experienced clinicians[21,107]

3. Teaching parents general principles of behavior management[21]

4. Addressing other factors besides parenting during treatment[49,107-109]

Unfortunately, studies of long-term treatment effects are few. However, several studies have found that some child behaviors learned through Parent Training continue over time.[110-112]

These programs build children's prosocial behavioral repertoires by:

1. Providing immediate and clear consequences for appropriate and inappropriate behaviors during school

2. Linking school behavior to home consequences via school-home cards

Although originally designed for children ages five through eight, aspects of each program can be easily adapted for use with older, elementary-school-aged children.

Both CLASS and RECESS last six to eight weeks, and each takes approximately 40 hours of direct contact time by the clinician.

Parents and teachers learn to communicate effectively using a simple system such as a school-home card.

School-Based Programs (CLASS and RECESS)

Many clinicians conduct treatment programs within the schools in an attempt to modify problematic behaviors that occur in the classroom or at recess. Two of the most well-developed and well-researched treatment packages for school-based behavior management are:

1. Contingencies for Learning Academic and Social Skills (CLASS)[113,114]

2. Reprogramming Environmental Contingencies for Effective Social Skills (RECESS).[113,115]

Basic Parameters. Clinicians conduct initial treatment sessions with an individual child in the classroom and on the play-ground. This serves a dual purpose. First, clinicians can model how to deliver the program for teachers and playground supervisors in the natural environment. Second, clinicians can demonstrate how well the program works when delivered correctly. During the later stages of the program, clinicians serve as consultants to teachers and/or playground supervisors as they administer the program.

CLASS Treatment Process. During the first five days, the clinician provides the child with continuous feedback about their behavior for several school periods each day. Using green and red cards to signal whether the child is behaving appropriately (green) or inappropriately (red), the clinician monitors the child's behavior throughout two, 20-to 30-minute periods. If the green card is displayed, the child receives a point and verbal praise every one to two minutes. If the red card is displayed, the child loses a point. If the child earns 80 percent of the possible points in a period, then the class earns a group-activity reward (e.g., the class is given five minutes of extra recess, the class gets to play a special game) immediately following the end of the period. The clinician documents the child's performance during both periods on a school-home behavior card.

The school-home card lists the biggest problems identified by the teacher. At the end of each class period, the clinician (and later the teacher) marks those problems that occurred. The child brings the card home at the end of the day, and the parents provide a consequence for appropriate (e.g., points and verbal reinforcement) or inappropriate (e.g., early bedtime) behavior. Parents also determine a consequence (e.g., no television) if the child fails to bring the contract home.

During days six through 20, the teacher administers the treatment program, using the red and green signaling cards intermittently, and fading them out completely by day 15. Parents and teachers gradually increase the magnitude of rewards at home and school as well as the interval required to earn each reward. For example, by day 16, the child must perform successfully for five days to earn a reward. During days 21 to 30, teachers and parents only give verbal praise or similar naturally occurring consequences as rewards.

Both parents and teachers should use brief time-outs to deal with negative behaviors.

RECESS Treatment Process. During the first few school days of the RECESS program, the clinician meets with parents, teachers, recess monitors, and the child to orient them to the program and explain each person's role. The clinician defines and models for the child exactly what differentiates positive social behaviors (e.g., maintaining eye contact, smiling, sharing) from negative ones (e.g., hitting, noncompliance). With the help of the child, the clinician then teaches these concepts to the entire class.

After reviewing playground rules, the clinician tells the children that the entire class will earn rewards for the child's appropriate behavior.

At this point, the clinician implements the behavioral program with the child during each recess period. At the beginning of each recess period, the child receives one point for each five-minute interval in the recess period (e.g., three points for a 15-minute period). The child is told to try to keep these points by interacting positively with others throughout the period and by following all playground rules.

The clinician provides ample verbal praise for the child's positive behaviors.

During this time, the child loses one point each time they act negatively toward another child or adult or each time they break a playground rule. The clinician tells the child each time a point is lost. If the child loses all points, they receive a Time Out for the remainder of recess. If the child behaves in an especially good manner or handles a difficult situation appropriately, a bonus point is awarded, which cannot be lost.

If the child retains a specific number of points across all recess periods in an entire day, the entire class participates in a fun group activity at the end of the school day.

During days 8 through 10, the recess supervisor administers the program under the direct supervision of the clinician and continues the program for three more weeks (days 11 through 25). The program also begins to operate in the classroom. In the classroom, the child receives regular praise for good behavior and earns access to recess by following classroom rules and interacting positively during academic periods immediately before recess. The child earns points at the beginning of

The school-home report card along with a home reward system is used to support the class program.

class and must retain them. Children who lose all points are not allowed to go to recess, and thus, lose the chance to earn points during recess for that period.

A naturally occurring reward might be allowing a child to accompany his or her parents to the grocery store as a reward for good behavior during the afternoon.

To monitor the progress of the child during treatment, clinicians encourage teachers to complete rating scales of child behaviors at frequent points and maintain a daily-record form summarizing the child's behavioral performance.

During the final phase (days 26 through 40), external controls, such as points and Time Outs, gradually fade to be replaced by verbal praise and other naturally occurring rewards both at home and at school.

Follow-up After Program Termination. These programs may be continued indefinitely, and the school-home behavior card can be an ongoing mechanism both to reinforce appropriate behavior at school and to keep communication open between teachers and parents.

What is the Effectiveness of School-Based Programs?

Both the CLASS and RECESS packages have been tested extensively using a variety of research designs.[113] Results indicate that while these programs are in effect, both reduce the negative social behaviors of children exhibiting conduct-disordered behaviors.

There is some evidence that the CLASS program has long-lasting effects. In two studies, children who received CLASS were utilizing significantly less special education services 18 to 36 months after program termination.[116]

Multidimensional Treatment Foster Care

When the juvenile court or a clinician and the family determine that an adolescent diagnosed with a conduct disorder needs an out-of-home placement, a promising alternative is Multidimensional Treatment Foster Care (MTFC).[72] The goals of MTFC are:

- To minimize the display of conduct-disordered behaviors
- To minimize the influence of deviant peers
- To encourage prosocial behaviors
- To promote the development of academic skills

Basic Parameters. Adolescents diagnosed with a conduct disorder are individually placed with foster parents who have been carefully screened and then trained to deliver the MTFC program. An adolescent spends an average of four to six months in foster care, during which time both they and their parents receive ongoing psychological interventions. A *case manager* supervises the entire intervention program, ensures that treatment goals are being met, and acts as the liaison between MTFC staff and external agencies, including the adolescent's school and the juvenile court. Case managers meet regularly with foster parents and clinicians and are on call 24 hours a day for crisis intervention.

case manager—a person, typically a social worker, who oversees all aspects of the client's treatment program

Treatment Process. Throughout the four- to six-month period, adolescents participate in individual therapy that focuses on social skills and problem solving skills (see Child Problem Solving Skills section in this chapter). Additionally, parents participate in Parent Training (see the Parent Training section of this chapter). Toward the middle of treatment, adolescents and parents meet together with both clinicians for family meetings. During these meetings, family members learn more positive ways of discussing important issues and solving problems together. These meetings help bridge the transition from foster care back to home.

*During TFC, the adolescent and the parents have **different** clinicians. An extremely important part of treatment is the building of supportive and trusting relationships between adolescent and clinician as well as between the parents and their clinician. These relationships form the base from which more difficult aspects of skills acquisition can be accomplished.*

During the program, foster parents use a three-level point system as the main vehicle to teach prosocial skills, reward appropriate behavior, and provide consequences for inappropriate behavior.

- **Level One**—a youth receives close supervision across all settings (e.g., home, school) and relatively immediate reinforcement. Points earned during one day lead to privileges received on the following day. Adolescents who do well can earn Level Two in two to three weeks.

All privileges must be earned, including phone time, free time, and allowance.

- **Level Two**—a youth is given more freedom and more delayed reinforcement. Points earned during one week lead to privileges received during the next week. All privileges must be earned, but more are available, including the chance to buy free time with friends.

All contacts with friends occur where the adolescent's whereabouts can be confirmed and monitored.

Adolescents can be demoted to Level One for low point days. If this happens, they must earn their way back to Level Two by gaining a certain number of points. To move to Level Three, even more points must be earned. For example, an adolescent must earn 12 bonds that cost 25 points each. One bond can be earned (purchased) per week. Adolescents usually stay at Level Two for three to four months.

All activities need to be approved, and the adolescent's whereabouts in the community continue to be followed closely.

- **Level Three**—a youth is given even more freedom. Rather than points being earned or lost, adolescents are rated globally each day on their performance of several behaviors. The ratings received determine the adolescent's allowance. Privileges do not have to be earned, but extra rewards can be earned for sustained appropriate behavior. Two or more low ratings for the same behavior on two consecutive days may result in a demotion to Level Two of up to one week. Official violations (e.g., police contacts) result in a demotion to Level One as well as other consequences.

One of the most important jobs of the therapist is to thoroughly convince the parents that they themselves must and can become experts at managing the behavior of their adolescent, often despite a long history of failed attempts.

Follow-up After Termination. MTFC "aftercare" services vary, depending on the needs of the adolescent and family. Clinicians hold parent group and individual sessions with parents to provide further information, assistance, and support in their efforts to manage their adolescent's behavior. Clinicians make frequent telephone contacts with parents to closely monitor the transition from MTFC to home. Clinicians may also hold individual sessions with adolescents to "coach" them in social and community relationship skills. *Respite care* services are provided for families if the parents and their adolescent need "a break" from each other. Other services, such as academic tutoring, can be provided or arranged as needed.

respite care—short-term out-of-home placements (e.g., a weekend)

What is the Effectiveness of Multidimensional Treatment Foster Care?

Researchers have examined MTFC efficacy in a sample of conduct-disordered male adolescents referred by the juvenile court.[117] In this study, youth randomly assigned to participate in MTFC had significantly fewer criminal referrals in the one-year period following treatment exit than those assigned to participate in services-as-usual group home programs.

For example, the percent of youths with at least one criminal referral during this period was 59 percent for those in an MTFC program and 93 percent for those in a group home. As predicted, the positive effect of MTFC over group homes on arrests was mediated by lower levels of deviant peer association and higher levels of monitoring, consistent discipline, and positive adult-youth relationships.[118] Researchers are conducting a similar study at the Oregon Social Learning Center with adolescent girls.

What is the Cognitive Therapy Approach to Treating the Conduct Disorders?

Children who have developed a repertoire of conduct-disordered behaviors also may have developed cognitive (thought) processes that are ineffective in prosocial situations.[119] For example, children who display aggressive behaviors tend to attribute hostile intentions to their peers even during neutral or ambiguous social interactions.[96] These tendencies have been labeled **social processing deficits**, and clinicians have observed that a variety of social processing deficits coincide with child aggressive behavior.[120] Unfortunately for the child, such "deficits" may actually be adaptive in some social settings in which they interact. However, they may be maladaptive in relatively benign situations.

Cognitive theorists believe that children unconsciously and rapidly process social behaviors in a way that leads to aggressive responses. They believe that a child perceives and reacts to a social stimulus based on how well aspects of that stimuli have predicted certain outcomes in previous encounters. If such stimuli have often been associated with threatening situations, the affective features most useful in determining a current threat will be attended to and other, less-predictive cues will be ignored.

Information (both process and outcome) of each processing sequence is thought to be stored in long-term-memory. The cumulative history that a child has with a particular stimulus is hypothesized to influence later processing.

For example, a peer frowns at a child. The child then interprets interactions (e.g., the peer's frown is interpreted as a threat. And the child feels a mix of fear and anger). Once the frown is interpreted as threatening, the child accesses an array of previously tried behavioral responses, such as:

- Running Away

- Pushing the peer

- Making a negative comment

- Frowning back

- Making no response

Social Information Processing psychologists hypothesize that cognitive processing errors serve as the immediate "cause" for observed aggressive behavior.[121]

The child evaluates and classifies each response as acceptable or unacceptable given the current situation. The sequence ends when the child exhibits the chosen response (e.g., swears at the peer, which likely starts a verbal argument and leads to a physical fight).

Although developed with elementary-school-aged children, Child Problem-Solving Skills Training can be adapted for older children.

conscious—in the person's awareness

Several researchers have found that bringing groups of children with problem behaviors together into group therapy settings may result in detrimental outcomes for individual group members (e.g., increases in the problem behaviors of group members).[127-129]

Session lengths vary, but usually do not exceed 75 minutes.

contingency management program—A system for rewarding good behaviors and providing costs for misbehaviors

What Treatment Methods Are Used With the Cognitive Approach?

In treating the conduct disorders, those who favor the cognitive approach use **Child Problem-Solving Skills Training** programs that focus on the development of adaptive ways to think through interpersonal problems.[122,123] The goal of this treatment is to make problem solving more *conscious*, proactive, and prosocial.

Basic parameters. Problem-solving skills can be taught individually or in small groups (e.g., five to 10 children). Many clinicians prefer small groups because:

1. Children can practice the skills with peers under the supervision of the clinician.

2. Group process can be used to facilitate change.[124]

Small groups usually include children of approximately the same age and/or developmental level and possibly of the same gender.[125] Groups may be limited to children with a conduct disorder or may include, a mix of children exhibiting different types of problems, children with and without a conduct disorder, or a "target" child's entire classroom. Current research provides no clear answers as to which group composition results in the most effective treatment.

Depending on the program, the number of sessions varies between 10 and 30, spread out over 10 to 20 weeks.[124-126] Some clinician/researchers hypothesize that the most ideal approach is to stretch training across an entire school year and then follow-up with periodic booster sessions. The longer time period provides children with more opportunity for skills rehearsal and may improve their ability to generalize their new skills to the natural environment.[125]

Session Content and Treatment Process. Clinicians conduct Problem-Solving Skills training programs in the context of a *contingency management program*. During the first meeting, clinicians present the rules for the group, provide participants with a list of the rules and consequences, post the rules, and role-play what will happen when the rules are broken.[126] They also detail rewards for appropriate behaviors, including tasks to be accomplished outside the session (i.e., "homework"). Subsequent meetings usually begin with a quick reminder of the rules. Through games, stories, and social interaction, children are taught to carefully analyze social problems using a methodical, step-by-step approach, such as:[124]

1. What is wrong?

2. What can I do?

3. Which choice is best?

Clinicians model the use of each step, observe children practicing the steps and give praise and correction as appropriate.

Problem-solving treatment sessions often include these steps:[125,126]

1. Review the group rules.

2. Verbally reinforce the child for the homework activities he or she completed during the past week.

3. Provide a brief, simple, and well-organized lecture on the topic of the day, emphasizing the precise steps needed to accomplish a specific goal. Supplement this talk with information on posters and handouts.

4. Preferably with a co-therapist, model the skills presented in the lecture during a role-play of a problem-solving situation.

5. With a child in front of the group, role-play a problem-solving situation to again demonstrate the skills presented; provide coaching and feedback.

6. In front of the group, provide coaching and feedback while two children use the target skills during a problem-solving role-play. If there are two therapists, this can be done by pairing each child with a therapist and having the therapists whisper corrective feedback as appropriate. Videotape this session if possible.

7. Review the role-play (using videotape, if available) and provide further feedback.

8. Briefly review the session.

9. Discuss weekly activities that the child can do to earn points towards rewards. To improve compliance, such tasks can be labeled "show that I can" rather than "homework".[133]

10. Provide any earned rewards.

Follow-up after Program Termination. Periodic booster sessions following treatment termination may promote the continued use of problem-solving skills as well as the generalization of these skills to new settings.[125] Using booster sessions is

A well thought out contingency management program that is properly introduced and consistently applied, greatly enhances the productivity of problem-solving skills training sessions. The contingency management program can also serve as a mechanism for providing approval, giving support, and (ultimately) building trust.

Modeling occurs throughout treatment sessions: the clinician not only formally demonstrates for the child how to solve problems in hypothetical situations, but uses problem solving skills as real problems arise during treatment.[126]

Treatment often includes other components (such as anger management) and basic social skills (such as group entry and play skills).[130-132]

During self-instruction training, clinicians coach children to talk themselves through problem-solving steps. A basic format for such training follows this sequence:[134]

1. Therapists role-play tasks while verbally (outloud) instructing themselves about what to do.

2. Children role-play the same situation while the therapist instructs them.

3. Children role-play the situation again, but this time instruct themselves out loud.

4. Children role-play the situation again, but whisper instructions to themselves.

5. Children role-play once more, while silently instructing themselves.

dysfunctional—patterns of behavior that have distressing and problematic outcomes

homeostasis—equilibrium or balance

conceptually appealing, but the effect of such on child behavior has not been studied.

What is the Effectiveness of the Cognitive Approach?

Problem-solving skills treatments appear to have some positive impacts on child aggressive behaviors, at least during and soon after treatment.[135] In several studies, children exhibiting aggressive behaviors were randomly assigned to Child Problem-Solving Skills Training, some other type of treatment, or a control group. After treatment, children in the Problem-Solving Skills condition have demonstrated greater decreases in aggressive behaviors than children in the other conditions.[124,130,136,137] How well these effects persist over time is unclear. Some studies indicate persistence of treatment effects up to one year after termination, while other studies indicate that many children fail to maintain treatment gains.[124,126,138]

What is the Family Therapy Approach to Treating Conduct Disorders?

In numerous studies, researchers have found that family factors, such as parent use of discipline, monitoring, and problem solving skills, significantly correlate with child antisocial behaviors.[12,97,139] In the Behavior Therapy model discussed previously, clinicians view all members of a child's nuclear family (or family system) as important players in the development of a conduct disorder. Family Therapy theorists also ascribe to this idea, and place the etiology, development, and maintenance of the child's problems primarily within the context of the family's verbal and nonverbal communication patterns.[140] According to these theorists, it is the *dysfunctional* family system, rather than the "identified patient" (i.e., the child diagnosed with a conduct disorder), that should be the focus of treatment. Other associated systems relevant to child and family behavior (e.g., the child's network of friends, the teachers and counselor at school, extended family) are also considered to be important in the maintenance of problems within the nuclear family, and thus attempts are made to systematically modify these systems as well.

Family theorists view a child's "conduct disorder" as one of a variety of problematic family symptoms that maintain *homeostasis* within a family system. The disorder is seen as a solution to some problem that currently threatens or once threatened to disrupt the accepted status-quo of the family.[132] For example, the primary family problem may be conflict between the parents that threatens the survival of the family. When the child diagnosed with a conduct disorder is misbehaving, parents may have to divert their focus away from their marital conflict. Thus, the disorder serves to keep the family together. Since curing the conduct disorder would require that the system respond with a "diversion" that might be equally undesirable, the only way to truly create useful change within the family is to change the family system.

Changing the family system requires:

1. Assessing what purposes maladaptive symptoms (e.g., child antisocial behavior) serve in the system

2. Then, changing family roles and communication and relationship patterns so that these purposes can be served in more adaptive ways

Despite the popularity of family therapy theories, sparse research exists on the outcome of family therapies for the conduct disorders.[142-244] However, preliminary supportive outcome data is available for Functional Family Therapy (FFT), and numerous studies have been conducted on Multisystemic Treatment (MST).

Functional Family Therapy

The primary goal of FFT is to improve and optimize communication within a family. Families are taught to convey their thoughts and feelings more clearly and precisely, to negotiate solutions to problems more effectively, and to use behavioral techniques to provide a more consistent home environment for their children.

Basic Parameters. This intervention was designed for children in early to mid-adolescence. All members of the family attend treatment sessions together. Sessions are held on a weekly basis and last for 60 minutes. Treatment continues until both the clinician and the family determine termination to be appropriate.

Theorists view healthy families as those in which family members give and receive clear and honest messages from each other.

Family roles describe the way that parents and children relate with one another in terms of power, allegiance, and function. Theorists view healthy families as those in which parents share power and decision making with each other and where there are clear boundaries between the parents (as a team) and other family members.

Communication patterns describe the way families verbally and non-verbally interact with each other on a day-to-day basis. Incongruent messages and other types of poor communication are considered both a cause and an effect of dysfunction within the family.[145]

Clinicians assist families in developing clearly defined parameters for child and family behavior. They learn to differentiate family rules (limits that must be followed) from family requests (statements that can be responded to either negatively or positively).

If one or more family members are unwilling to address the major problem immediately, families negotiate a minor issue (e.g., performing a chore at home) and later progress to major issues.

A secondary focus of treatment is on helping families develop a token economy system to reward desired child and family behaviors (see the Parent Training and Treatment Foster Care sections).

recidivism—relapse rate (e.g., getting arrested again)

Treatment Process. During treatment, the clinician models, shapes, and teaches the family communication skills within the context of ongoing family problem-solving discussions. The process typically follows this pattern:

1. The clinician gives family members reading assignments that introduce social learning principles. (See Parent Training for Parents in the Appendix.)

2. Through observing and interviewing the family, the clinician learns about family interactions that seem to be related to the child's conduct-disordered behaviors. The clinician uses this knowledge to help shape the family's problematic interactions into more kind and productive encounters.

3. From the first session, the family works on negotiating solutions to those family problems that the clinician hypothesizes are related to the child's conduct-disordered behaviors. The clinician actively models clear, efficient, and adaptive communication skills, and prompts and reinforces these skills with family members during the negotiation. Throughout negotiations, clinicians frequently state their hypotheses about the meaning of and purposes for various verbal and nonverbal communications used by family members. Family members are encouraged to correct and clarify these interpretations.

4. During continued negotiations, the clinician teaches the family a variety of skills to improve the communication clarity between family members.

Follow-up After Program Termination. Booster sessions can be added as needed to fine-tune communication within the family.

What is the Effectiveness of Functional Family Therapy?

There is preliminary support for the efficacy of FFT. In a well-cited study, families with children who had been detained by police for several relatively low-level offenses (e.g., running away; being declared "ungovernable"; being habitually truant; shoplifting; or possessing tobacco, drugs, or alcohol) were randomly assigned to several conditions, including FFT. Relative to a no-treatment control group and two "community-standard" treatment groups, children whose families participated in the FFT condition had lower *recidivism* rates for these low-level offenses six to 18 months after treatment.[146]

Unfortunately, the average number of serious criminal offenses (e.g., robbery, burglary) committed remained constant for all treatment groups. In a follow-up study, siblings within the FFT-treated families also had lower rates of police detainment for any offense 30 to 42 months after treatment.[147]

Multisystemic Treatment

In contrast to the exclusive family focus in Functional Family Therapy, Multisystemic Treatment (MST) focuses on modifying any system (e.g., family, school, peer, community) important in maintaining the child's conduct-disordered behaviors.[149] The primary goal of treatment is to provide parents with the skills and resources needed to independently address the challenges presented by their children.

Basic Parameters. MST was designed to be delivered to adolescents and their families. Nuclear family members, extended family members, peers, teachers, neighbors, community center staff, and other pertinent figures in a child's life all may be involved in treatment. Clinicians meet with families in whatever location and at whatever time is most convenient for the family (often in the evenings at the family's home). Sessions usually last between 15 and 90 minutes and may occur daily. Treatment continues until a reasonable level of functioning has been achieved by the child and parents. The average duration of treatment is four months, and average contact time for the clinician is 30 hours.

Treatment Process. MST treatment generally proceeds as follows:

1. The clinician schedules the initial meeting in the family's home. During that meeting, each family member discusses the presenting problem and associated issues. The clinician helps the family clarify problems, assesses family strengths that could assist in alleviating problems, and helps the family set reasonable immediate and long-term goals. An action-oriented plan is developed to meet an immediate goal, giving family members and the clinician explicit, reasonable, and daily tasks to accomplish the plan.

2. While family members are working on the initial plan, the clinician contacts the child's school administrator and teachers, the child's peers, and/or extended family members to further assess the problem and search for possible solutions available within the existing systems.

The most recent revision of FFT includes several additions to the basic communication skills program (e.g., cognitive interventions targeting inappropriate perceptions that family members hold about each other).[148] The effectiveness of this revised treatment package has not yet been tested.

Clinicians view MST as a "family-preservation" intervention since they use this therapy to treat children diagnosed with Conduct Disorder who are at imminent risk for being institutionalized due to chronic delinquent behavior.

Across the course of treatment, clinicians are available 24 hours a day, seven days a week for intervention activities.

Clinicians address both the basic psychological and seemingly "non-psychological" needs of the family (e.g., child care, transportation).

For example, if the family's basic physical needs are not currently being met, the first goal might be to obtain necessary services and materials (e.g., food, child care, transportation, and medical care). To accomplish this, the clinician would help the family link up with available resources in the community.

If peers contribute to the child's problem, clinicians may emphasize pursuing new friendships, and follow this by trying to involve children in activities where relationships with prosocial peers can be fostered.

3. After addressing basic needs, the clinician uses Parent Training (see pages 31-39), Child Problem-Solving Skills Training (see, pages 46-48), Community and School Interventions (see pages 40-44), and other psychological interventions as appropriate. These interventions should build skills and effect changes that promote positive, pervasive, and lasting treatment effects. The primary goal is to focus on the family's present problems. However, problems related to past events are acknowledged and dealt with if possible (e.g., by providing restitution).

The clinician may work with the child during individual therapy on remedying problem-solving skill deficits or may simply provide emotional support for the child during the treatment process.

4. Family sessions are held regularly throughout treatment. During each session, the clinician probes family members on their efforts to accomplish assigned tasks and gives ample praise if the tasks were completed. If tasks were not completed, the clinician attempts to discern why not and develop a new plan. When families fail to accomplish treatment goals in a reasonable amount of time (i.e., two to three weeks), alternative plans should be made and put into place immediately. Sessions conclude with the assignment of tasks to each participant.

5. Across the course of treatment, clinicians develop interventions both within and between each system (e.g., family, school, peers) as appropriate. In addition, clinicians assess and monitor the child's behavior within each system on a continuous basis.

Follow-up After Program Termination. Booster sessions can be conducted to address further issues as needed.

What is the Effectiveness of MST?

To date, numerous studies have examined the effectiveness of MST.[150] For example, adolescents with "serious" juvenile offense records were randomly assigned to MST or traditional services (i.e., probation with various stipulations). Relative to the traditional services group, adolescents who received MST were detained by police fewer times, reported committing less offenses, and spent less time incarcerated. However, the only highly significant treatment effect was a shorter duration of incarceration (on average, 10 weeks less).[151] In another study, adolescents with extensive offense records were randomly assigned to MST or "eclectic" (psychodynamic, client-centered, and/or behavioral) individual therapy.[152] Recidivism approximately five years later was 22 percent for those who completed treatment in the MST group and 71 percent for those who completed individual therapy. Ratings on various other measures tended to favor the MST group.

Each of these studies suffers from several methodological flaws, but MST does appear promising. Additional treatment outcome studies are currently in progress, and the results may provide more definitive information on treatment efficacy.[153]

What is the Group Therapy Approach to Treating Conduct Disorders?

As previously discussed, theorists hypothesize that peer groups (particularly deviant peer groups) play a prominent role in the "basic training" of antisocial behavior in children (and adolescents in particular) as well as in the long-term maintenance of such behaviors.[12] The most well known group therapy to effect change in conduct-disordered behaviors is Child Problem-Solving Skills Training (see pages 46-48).

There are two recommended Group Therapy Approaches this section addresses that attempt to use the group setting to leverage change in the child's conduct-disordered behaviors:

1. Community Center–Based Group Treatment derived from the theories underlying Behavior Therapy and Family Therapy

2. The Day Camp-Based Group Treatment based on the theoretical persuasions of Behavior Therapy and Cognitive Therapy

Community Center-Based Group Treatment

Deviant peer groups play a prominent role in the display of conduct-disordered behaviors, particularly when parents or other adults do not supervise contact with deviant peers. Based on this finding, researchers have hypothesized that minimizing contact with deviant peers and maximizing contact with prosocial peers in supervised settings likely decreases conduct-disordered behaviors. Further, treatment provided in "unstigmatized" settings, such as a community center, may result in greater success than treatment confined to clinical settings.[154]

Basic Parameters. Community Center-Based Group Treatment was designed for all school-aged children.[84,154] Children participate in groups of 10 to 15. Groups comprise children without behavior problems who attend after-school activity programs at a community center as part of their regular schedule, as well as one or two children who exhibit conduct-disordered behaviors. The groups meet once a week for two to three hours throughout the school year.

Major activities involve planning and participating in various recreational activities at the community center. Staff members teach problem-solving skills and other prosocial behaviors during group activities on both a formal and informal basis.

53

Social Learning treatments use the same basic techniques, discussed in the Parent Training section on pages 31-39.

Treatment Process. Community Center-Based Group Treatment utilizes two basic group approaches: Social Learning and Traditional. In Social Learning groups, clinicians systematically apply individual and group contingencies to reward desired behaviors and discourage undesired behaviors. Clinicians use shaping, modeling, role-playing, and coaching to teach prosocial behaviors. In addition, they engage in continuous assessment of individual behaviors to check intervention effectiveness, and make changes in the treatment plan based on these results.

Traditional groups reflect social psychological and social group work principles similar to the conceptualizations used in Family Therapy. The clinician focuses on rules, norms, and consequences, helping leaders emerge, and the mechanisms the group uses to solve problems. Traditional groups do not use the contingencies employed by Social Learning groups.

Follow-up After Program Termination. Groups are conducted throughout each school year, and can be continued during the summer (see the following section).

What is the Effectiveness of Community Center-Based Group Therapy?

Insight-oriented Group Therapy has been advanced for the conduct disorders, but these types of treatments have not been found effective.[142]

One of the best examples of a controlled treatment outcome study of group intervention is the St. Louis Experiment. That study contrasted the efficacy of three treatment methods (Social Learning, Traditional, and Control/Minimal).[83] The study also examined two other factors: the clinician's experience level (low and high) and group composition (mixed and unmixed).

In mixed groups, one or two randomly chosen children who displayed conduct-disordered behaviors were assigned to a group of nine to 14 children who did not display such problems. Unmixed groups were comprised of 10 to 15 randomly chosen children who displayed conduct-disordered behaviors.

Regardless of the treatment method to which the child was assigned, children who were in mixed groups displaying conduct-disordered behaviors appeared to fare better than those who were in unmixed groups, especially if the groups were led by experienced leaders. This is an extremely important finding, since it is common for children who display similar problem behaviors to be grouped together away from prosocial peers to receive various interventions.

Other studies also report negative effects when children with problem behaviors are grouped together for "treatment."[128,129] For example, a recent study of adolescents "at risk" for substance use and other problem behaviors contrasted the effectiveness of a group Parent Training intervention, a peer-group intervention, and a Parent Training/peer-group combined intervention. After treatments, those who received the peer-group intervention used more tobacco and were rated by teachers as having more behavior problems than children who received no intervention.[129]

Day Camp-Based Group Treatment

Summer is a time when many children have large amounts of unstructured and unsupervised time. Unfortunately, children diagnosed with a conduct-disorder tend to commit problem behaviors when they are in unstructured and unsupervised situations, especially during adolescence. One promising, summertime treatment option that addresses this and other problems is a structured, day-camp treatment program. Several versions of these programs have been proposed, and some have been under development for many years.[155] The **Summer Treatment Program (STP)** was developed as a treatment for children with ADHD. Many of these children have also been diagnosed with a conduct disorder. STP's main goal is to improve a child's ability to effectively relate in a prosocial manner with other children and adults in a variety of settings.

The STP is an intense treatment program focusing on minimizing a child's negative behaviors and increasing a child's positive behavioral repertoire.

Basic Parameters. Children participate with a group of 10 to 12 age-matched children from 8:00 a.m. to 5:00 p.m. weekdays for eight weeks during the summer. The STP utilizes the computers, classrooms, gymnasium, and playing fields of an entire elementary school.

The program was originally designed for children in elementary school, but has recently been extended to children in early- to mid-adolescence.

In contrast to the other treatment programs discussed (which are often delivered via an individual clinician), the STP utilizes a large staff. Ideally, each 10- to 12-person group of children requires five direct service counselors, including one "lead counselor" at the masters or doctoral-level. A licensed psychologist supervises the direct service team. Elementary and secondary school teachers, a nurse, and a consulting psychiatrist are also on staff. The success of the program depends heavily on a low staff-to-child ratio.

Treatment Process. The STP focuses on developing academic, sports, and social skills as well as children's individual and group problem-solving skills. All aspects of the program, including skills training and time-out procedures, are tailored to be developmentally appropriate for each age-matched group of children (e.g., Time Outs are longer for older children than

Peer relationship skills are also taught within the context of a "buddy system." Children are paired up, and parents are encouraged to get the children together outside of camp.

younger). Each day, children participate in classroom experiences, including:

- Computer-assisted education, art instruction, and academic instruction

- Instruction on sports rules (e.g., soccer, baseball, basketball) and intensive coaching and supervised practice in sports skills

- Group problem-solving discussions and role-playing

- Constant instruction, modeling, and practice of appropriate problem-solving and social skills

Children tend to view the STP as an enjoyable experience rather than as a "treatment program." Embedding the treatment within a summer camp context serves to normalize the experience.

Treatment Process. Children participate with their group in a variety of skill training and field trip activities each day. A camp-wide token reinforcement program, or point system, is used throughout the summer to reward appropriate behaviors and provide consequences for inappropriate behavior. For example, points are given for following rules, sharing, and ignoring provocation. Points are lost for swearing, interrupting, and physical aggression. Points earned in the system can be exchanged for privileges, honors, and/or parent-provided rewards. Besides a loss of points, children receive Time Outs immediately following misbehaviors. Initially, children receive relatively long Time Outs (e.g., 30 minutes). However, the length of the Time Out is reduced if a child behaves appropriately during Time Out (e.g., from 30 to 10 minutes).

A clinical staff member, whose sole purpose is to tally points, tracks child behaviors on a moment-by-moment basis. Other clinical staff members "call in" points to the point recorder as they are earned or lost.

Parents participate in debriefing sessions at the end of each day, attend group Parent Training sessions once a week, and receive regular phone calls about treatment progress.

Parents learn basic principles of behavior management during an eight-week, one-day-per-week group Parent Training program.

Follow-up After Program Termination. The STP was designed to be part of a comprehensive, year-round, long-term treatment program.[155] During the school year, Parent Training continues as needed, and children participate in a one-day-per-week version of the STP called the Saturday Treatment Program.

What is the Effectiveness of STP?

Parents, teachers, and camp counselor ratings of child problem behavior all tend to improve following the STP. Further, treatment dropout tends to be quite low.[155] However, neither the short-term nor the long-term impact of the STP has yet been examined in a controlled investigation. The STP was one of several components in the psychosocial treatment package for the National Institute of Mental Health-sponsored Multimodal

Treatment study. This study examined the effectiveness of various types of intervention conditions (i.e., psychosocial only, medication only, psychosocial and medication combined, and a "services-as-usual" control) for children diagnosed with ADHD.[156,157] Fourteen months of psychosocial treatment produced positive results for 67% of participants for symptoms of aggression, anxiety, social skills, inattention, and hyperactive-impulsive behavior. [158-162]

What is the Psychodynamic Approach to Treating the Conduct Disorders?

Psychodynamic theorists who have spent the most time researching the conduct disorders are the Attachment theorists. The fundamental tenet of Attachment theory is that feelings of security and control elicited by infant-mother separations and reunions give rise to "cognitive-affective" schema, or "working models," of both the self, others, and the relationship between self and others.[163,164] For example, an infant who does not experience consistent attention may develop a schema that people are not to be trusted. Once established, theorists hypothesize that these schema influence the growing child's perceptions, cognitions, and motivations. This influence modifies the way the child responds to the behaviors of others. Thus, these schema are viewed as important influences on the way an individual interprets and responds to other's behaviors throughout life.[165] According to this theory, nonresponsive, insensitive caregiving during infancy leads to the development of "insecure" attachment schema, which, in turn, makes a child particularly vulnerable to exhibiting conduct-disordered behaviors.[166]

What Treatment Methods are Used with the Psychodynamic Approach?

Despite the success of Parent Training, Attachment theorists have criticized the approach for ignoring the causal importance of underlying beliefs. Attachment theorists claim that most of what Parent Training really changes is appearances, or "surface structure." The real problems, they hypothesize, reside in the "deep structure" of cognitions inside the child's mind, and these are not changed as a result of Parent Training. Furthermore, in parent-child relationships where there are severe problems (such as physical abuse of the child), Attachment theorists argue that helping the parent learn ways to gain

In developmental psychology, the word "attachment" refers to a set of contact-seeking behaviors exhibited by all infants during the later part of the first year of life. During this period, infants become wary of strangers, and become distressed and cry when separated from their mothers (or the infants' primary caregivers). When infants are once again in physical contact with their mothers, their distress tends to subside.

Insecure children tend to use conflictual or coercive behaviors as their primary means of regulating caretaking behaviors, which are likely to initiate the parent-child coercive interactions typical of conduct-disordered behaviors. (See the discussion of Behavioral Theory on page 30.)

further control of their child's behavior is probably unwise, even if the new techniques are nonviolent. Rather, theorists contend that, first and foremost, these parents need to learn to relinquish some of their control over their child. The Dyadic Skills Training Program, an enhanced version of a basic Parent Training program, was designed for parents of noncompliant young children (ages three to eight years) and attempts to remedy the deficiencies Attachment theorists ascribe to Parent Training programs.[166]

Dyadic Skills Training Program

Basic Parameters. The program was designed for preschool aged children and their parents who attend all treatment sessions together. Hour-long sessions are held in the clinic on a weekly basis for 12 to 18 weeks.

Treatment Process. The first stage of treatment is the Assessment Phase (two-three sessions). In addition to the assessment strategies discussed in chapter two, the clinician probes the history and status of the parent-child attachment relationship and as well as the attachment history of the parent (usually the mother) with his or her parents. The clinician observes several separation and reunion situations (e.g., mother leaves child alone in room for several minutes, then returns) and notes the behaviors and emotional expressions that occur during the separations and reunions.

After assessment, Dyadic Skills Training is recommended when:

1. Attachment issues are clearly a problem for the parent and child (e.g., exerting control is the most prominent parent behavior observed).

2. Parents clearly have difficulty demonstrating positive, accepting feelings toward the child.

During treatment the clinician teaches parents about the normative social, cognitive, and emotional development of preschoolers, and explains the tendency for preschoolers to attempt to be independent and autonomous from parents. From this context, clinicians reframe parent difficulties as a problematic juggling act between closeness, autonomy, and limit setting. The child's difficulties are reframed as part of the natural tendencies of growing up.

Next, the clinician attempts to facilitate an elevation in the child's level of control in the parent-child relationship by increasing unstructured, undirected, parent-child play that occurs

Parent and child are observed and behaviors noted during child-directed and parent-directed play, particularly behaviors relating to discipline or "control" issues.

Clinicians frame treatment as a process that will help improve the parent-child relationship.

in the family, and by training the parent how to play in a way that yields control to the child. Parent-child play sessions are usually videotaped. The clinician and parent watch the videotapes together, and the clinician uses instruction, modeling, role-playing, and coaching to teach parents better ways to respond (or not respond) to their child. The videotapes of play can also be used to elicit the parent's cognitive (e.g., "Chris does that on purpose to make me mad"), and affective reactions (e.g., "Chris has a quick temper"), to their child's behaviors and to help parents think from their children's perspectives.

Elevating the child's level of control provides a more constructive way for parents and children to communicate. This way of relating may be quite a contrast to the negative discipline confrontations that they have likely been enduring for some time.

Parents learn limit setting through "standard" Parent Training with a focus on using the least restraint possible to maintain order. The clinician helps parents sort their child's negative behaviors into low-level, ignorable behaviors (e.g., whining) and harmful behaviors (e.g., hitting, leaving the house). The clinician encourages parents to reduce limit setting attempts on ignorable behavior and to be firm on limit setting for harmful behavior. Further, parents learn indirect methods for most limit setting. These include:

Clinicians regularly give homework assignments that include parent reframing exercises such as "Chris isn't doing that just to make me mad. She likes playing video games more than taking out the trash".

- Using natural consequences
- Using "when/then" contingencies (i.e., "When you do this first, then you can do that.")
- Providing choices for the child that coincide with the parent's desires
- Offering specific, labeled praise for positive behaviors

In addition, parents and children receive homework assignments for practicing problem-solving skills while they make minor decisions or negotiate day-to-day departures and reunions. As their skills improve, they are assigned more stressful situations to negotiate.

Follow-up After Program Termination. Clinicians can make a six-month follow-up phone call to check on the child's progress with both the parents and the child's teacher. At this point, further treatment can be pursued if indicated.

What is the Effectiveness of the Psychodynamic Approach?

Neither the short-term nor the long-term impact of this treatment package has been investigated. However, some evidence exists regarding the efficiency of the Parent Training component of the program (see Parent Training on page 31).

Some version of play therapy is a more common psychodynamic approach to treating children diagnosed with a conduct disorder. Available scientific evidence does not indicate this type of therapy to be effective in reducing antisocial behavior.[167]

What are the Biological Influences and Treatments for the Conduct Disorders?

neurotransmitters—chemical agents that carry information between nerve cells in the body and affect behavior, mood, and thoughts

hypothalamus—a brain structure involved in the control of body temperature, heart rate, blood pressure, etc.

amygdala—a brain structure that plays a role in emotional behavior such as aggression, motivation, and memory functions

Despite the lack of scientific research on biological causes of the conduct disorders, there has been extensive biological research on aggression, one important symptom of the conduct disorders. Researchers have identified a variety of *neurotransmitters* (e.g., serotonin, norepinephrine) and brain structures (e.g., *hypothalamus , amygdala*), that appear to be related to the display of aggressive behaviors.[142,168] Ample evidence exists that aggressive behavior can be biologically induced (e.g., via physical injury, illness, removal of brain tissue, organic syndromes) and modified (e.g., via hormones, food deprivation, electrical stimulation, medications) to varying degrees in both animals and humans.[168]

Spurred on by these findings, researchers have investigated whether a tendency to display conduct-disordered behaviors is genetically transmitted across human generations. In the most relevant of these studies, researchers have examined the co-occurrence of criminal behavior (a legal designation, rather than a scientific one) among relatives, rather than the co-occurrence of a formally diagnosed conduct disorder. Based on the results of several studies, at least some differences in criminal behavior can be attributed to genetic factors.[169-172] However, in several other studies of similar quality, differences in criminal behavior are more attributable to environmental factors.[167,173,174]

Despite these mixed findings, a popular hypothesis for how genetic factors might influence the development of a conduct disorder early in life is through inherited tendencies to display inattentive, impulsive, and hyperactive behaviors.[25,175-177] Such behaviors probably contribute to difficulties in parent-child interactions, which in turn could lead to the coercive family processes that Behavioral theorists believe teach children a repertoire of antisocial behaviors. (See pages 30.) Such an interaction between a child's genetic predisposition and their environment seems to be the most plausible explanation for how genetic factors might be related to the conduct disorders.[178]

How are Medications Used to Treat the Conduct Disorders?

Medication is not used as the primary treatment for any of the conduct disorders. Rather, medications may be used to decrease severe and extreme aggressive behavior. The most common types of medications used to treat severe aggression are Lithium and the neuroleptics. Medication is also used to treat related problems such as Attention Deficit Hyperactivity Disorder (ADHD). *Stimulants* are the most common medications used to treat co-occurring ADHD and conduct disorders. Prescribing medications is indicated only by the presence of ADHD, but the treatment may impact favorably on some conduct-disordered symptoms (e.g., aggression, noncompliance). Pages 64-67 lists these medications as well as dosage and side effects.

The stimulants are by far the most likely psychotropic class of medications that the clinician will encounter for treating children with conduct disorders. This is due to the high co-occurence of ADHD with the conduct disorders and the high frequency that physicians prescribe stimulant treatment for ADHD symptoms.

On any given day, at least 750,000 children are given a stimulant.[179]

The Stimulants

The stimulants are the most common *psychotropic* medications prescribed for children in the United States.[180] Three commonly prescribed stimulants are methylphenidate, dextro-amphetamine, and pemoline.[181] Caffeine is an even more common stimulant, but caffeine is not considered effective in managing either ADHD or the conduct disorders.[182]

Pharmacology —The chemical structure of the stimulants closely resembles the structure of the neurotransmitters in the nervous system. Stimulants appear to act by:

1. Increasing the release of dopamine and norepinephrine (neurotransmitters in the brain) into the *synapse*

2. Blocking the *reuptake* of dopamine and norepinephrine[183]

The net effect of these changes appears to be the enhancement of the sensitivity of the central nervous system to stimulation.[73] Researchers have not yet determined exactly what area of the brain is most important for the effect of stimulants on conduct-disordered and attention-deficit-disordered behaviors; however, the frontal cortex and the striatum are likely involved.[180,184]

stimulant—*a medication that increases the arousal of the Central Nervous System*

psychotropic—*broadly, a substance that impacts on the behavior, emotions, and/ or thoughts of an individual*

synapse—*the space between individual nerve cells in the brain*

reuptake—*reabsorption of a neurotransmitter into the cell that released it*

Treatment: Standard Medication Trial. Ideally, standard treatment with a stimulant medication follows several distinct phases:

- Pre-medication assessment (e.g., two weeks of baseline information on the problem behaviors)

- Medication titration

- Maintenance

- Re-evaluation

Although there are no clear long-term negative effects of stimulant treatments, the lowest possible effective dosage is most desirable.

Determining the optimal dose requires a careful weighing of positive treatment effects and adverse side effects. For example, a child's behavioral problems may be impacted significantly at a dose of 0.6 mg/kg/day, but adverse cognitive effects as well as bothersome side effects may be present. To adequately contrast costs and benefits, data on cognitive-behavioral performance and side effects should be collected frequently throughout the *titration* period from parents, teachers, and children at each dosage level.[48] The titration period ends when clinicians determine what dose seems most appropriate.

titration—slow increase in medication until significant effects on the problem behaviors are noticed

During maintenance, adjustments can be made in the timing of pill ingestion so that the therapeutic effects of the stimulant coincide with the need for maximum symptom control.[184] Sometimes, slow release pills or additional low doses are added to circumvent *behavioral rebound* or drug withdrawal symptoms. Children are sometimes given "medication holidays" on the weekends and during the summer, especially if the child is experiencing adverse effects due to the stimulants.

behavioral rebound—an exaggeration of presenting symptoms five to 15 hours after the last dose of stimulants

Clinicians should evaluate (through feedback from child, parents, and teachers) whether or not to continue stimulant use every six to 12 months.[48,180,184] *Tolerance* to methylphenidate may develop if treatment continues beyond one year. If tolerance does seem to be an issue and continued treatment is indicated, clinicians can try prescribing other stimulants.[185]

tolerance—diminished responsiveness to a drug due to repeated use, thus requiring larger doses to have the same effect

Treatment: Double-Blind Placebo-Controlled Medication Trial. While standard psychiatric practice utilizes some form of medication titration, a more preferable strategy is the double-blind, placebo-controlled trial strategy. This strategy more clearly reveals the usefulness of stimulant treatment for a given child.[186-188] During a double-blind trial, neither the clinician, parent(s), teachers, or child know what type of pill the child is receiving each day. Thus, the trial has built in controls for the "placebo effect" (i.e., symptoms improving simply because the child receives a pill, regardless of what the pill

There is some debate about whether true tolerance develops or whether dose changes are needed simply because of weight increase as children mature.[185]

contains). Each day of the medication trial (generally four days each week for four to six weeks), a child randomly receives either a placebo (i.e., sugar pill) or one of several different dosages of medication (e.g., 0.3 mg/kg/day and 0.6 mg/kg/day of Ritalin).[185]

During the trial, the clinician collects data on problem behaviors and side effects daily from teachers, parents, and the child. At the end of the trial, the clinician computes and compares results for each problem behavior under each pill type.[186] In most cases, this data will clearly indicate which dose improves and stabilizes the child's performance. If no differences exist across medication conditions, or if medication side effects are problematic, alternative stimulants can be investigated using a similar format.

Standard Medication Trial vs. Double-Blind Placebo-Controlled Medication Treatment.
No studies have been done that directly compare treatment decisions made during a medication titration trial and double-blind, placebo-controlled trial. Within programs that routinely do high-quality, double-blind trials, less than 50 percent of children with diagnoses of ADHD received definite recommendations for continued stimulant treatment.[186] It is unclear whether this seemingly low rate of recommendation for stimulant treatment (in the context of the precipitously high prescription rate of stimulants in the United States) is due to the use of double-blind procedures or to the concurrent, intensive psychosocial interventions operating within these programs.

During a double-blind trial, pills are placed within identical, opaque gelatin capsules to mask their identity, and then prepackaged in pill boxes that clearly label the appropriate pills for each day and time.

Concurrent, intensive psychosocial treatment tends to reduce the amount of stimulant medication needed to show improvement.[189]

Figure 3.1 — *Psychotropic Medications Used To Manage*

Name and Type	Target Symptoms	Dosage
Name: Methylphenidate Hydrochloride (Ritalin, Metadate, Methylin, Concerta) **Type**: Stimulant	Inattention, impulsivity, hyperactivity, mild aggression, noncompliance	**Target range:** 0.15 to 0.6 mg/kg/day or 2.5 to 25 mg/day. **Maximum:** 2.0 mg/kg/day or 60 mg/day or 20 mg/dose **Number of doses:** 1 to 3 per day. Often 8 a.m., 12 noon, and smaller afternoon dose if behavioral rebound or drug withdrawal a problem. If slow release (SR) capsules used, one dose in a.m. with possible additional small quick-release dose in p.m. **Treatment response:** Within 30 to 60 minutes post ingestion. Peaks at 1 to 2 hours, dissipates at 2 to 5 hours. With slow release, peak at 1 to 4 hours, dissipates at 2 to 12 hours.
Name: Dextroamphetamine Sulfate (Dexedrine and Dextrostat) **Type**: Stimulant	Inattention, impulsivity, hyperactivity, mild aggression, noncompliance	**Target range:** 0.1 to 0.3 mg/kg/day (up to 1.0 mg/kg/day) or 2.5 to 20 mg/day. **Maximum:** 40 mg/day or 10 mg/dose. **Number of doses:** 1 to 3 per day. Spansule (i.e., slow release) 1 per day. **Treatment response:** Similar to methylphenidate.
Name: Magnesium Pemoline (Cylert and Pemolert) **Type**: Stimulant	Inattention, impulsivity, hyperactivity, mild aggression, noncompliance	**Target range:** 0.5 to 3.0 mg/kg/day or 18.75 to 112.5 mg/day. **Maximum:** 112.5 mg/day. **Number of doses:** 1 per day. **Treatment response**: May be up to 3 to 4 weeks until treatment effect observed, then within 30 to 60 minutes post ingestion. Peak effect 1 to 4 hours, dissipates after 7 to 8 hours.
Name: Desimpramine Hydro-chloride (Norpramin) **Type**: Tricyclic antidepressant	Inattention, impulsivity, hyperactivity, mild aggression, noncompliance	**Target range:** 0.5 to 2.5 mg/kg/day or 20 to 100 mg/day. Final dosage depends on serum level. Monitor serum during treatment to check if therapeutic levels are being maintained. **Maximum:** 5 mg/kg/day, not exceeding 300mg/day. **Number of doses**: 2 to 3 per day for pre-adolescents (e.g., 8 a.m., 4 p.m., bedtime); one dose/day for adolescents at bedtime. **Treatment response:** Development and maintenance of drug "steady state" required. Generally, steady state achieved in 3 to 4 days, treatment effects appear later.
Name: Clonidine Hydrochlo-ride (Catapres or Catapres-TTS) **Type**: Antihypertensive	Inattention, impulsivity, hyperactivity, mild aggression, noncompli-ance; may be best for hyperaroused child, with high levels of motor activity and aggression	**Target range:** 3 to 4 g/kg/day or 0.1 to 0.3 mg/day. **Maximum**: 0.3 mg/day. **Number of doses:** 1-2. Available in skin patch (TTS). **Treatment response:** With oral dose, within 1 hour post inges-tion. Peak effects 3 to 5 hours. With skin patch, 2 to 3 days to reach therapeutic levels.

Conduct Disorder and Related Symptoms

Common Side Effects	**Special Concerns**
Insomnia, decreased appetite, weight loss, stomachaches, headaches, irritability. A variety of other side effects possible, including behavioral rebound, dizziness, agitation, apprehension, dysphoria, moodiness, increased heart rate, increased systolic blood pressure, anorexia, nausea. Appears to decrease growth in weight, but not growth in height, although impact on height is possible. Possible drug withdrawal symptoms (e.g., extreme fatigue, anxiety, depression) late in day after last dose dissipates or if abrupt cessation of treatment. Abuse potential. Drug does have euphoric properties, although less than dextroamphetamine.	Do not use with children under 6 years. Not advisable to use concurrently with other psychotropic drugs. Simultaneous use may elevate levels of both drugs (e.g., with tricyclic antidepressants, anticonvulsants). Concurrent use with monoamine oxidase inhibitors may elevate blood pressure to dangerous levels. Can interfere with the actions of a variety of other non-psychotropic medications. Use with oral steroids (for asthma) can result in dizziness, tachycardia, palpitation, weakness, agitation. Use with antihistamines may decrease effectiveness of stimulant. Side effects may be greater in children with low IQ. Generally thought to be contraindicated if history of tics and/or family history of Tourette's syndrome, although treatment may be pursued with caution. Use with caution if co-occurring seizure disorder or high blood pressure. Other contraindications include concurrent psychosis; marked agitation, tension, or anxiety; glaucoma; family members at risk for abusing and/or selling stimulants.
Side effects similar to methylphenidate. Decrease in weight velocity may be greater than methylphenidate. Most euphoric of stimulants.	Do not use with children less than 3 years. Other issues similar to methylphenidate.
Similar to methylphenidate. **Insomnia** may be a particular problem. Least euphoric of stimulants.	Do not use with children less than 6 years. Other issues similar to methylphenidate.
Dry mouth, decreased appetite, headaches, tiredness, dizziness, insomnia. Also increased heart rate, increased diastolic blood pressure, weight loss. Many other side effects possible, including cardiac problems. When drug treatment terminated, especially if abruptly, severe flu-like symptoms (e.g., stomach pains, fever, malaise) possible.	Use with extreme caution in children less than 12 years. Three recent deaths during or following exercise of elementary school-aged children being treated with this drug. Concurrent use with stimulants elevates levels of both drugs. Do not use concurrently with a monoamine oxidase inhibitor. Concurrent use of antiasthmatic medications or caffeine may be a problem. Overheating may be a problem, so caution should be taken during exercise, hot weather. Contraindicated if family history of sudden cardiac death.
Sedation, nausea, vomiting, headache, dizziness, rash with skin patch. Variety of other side effects including dry mouth, vomiting, weight gain, nervousness, agitation, orthostatic hypotension, cardiovascular problems, kidney problems, fatigue, depression, cardiac arrhythmias. Sudden termination of treatment may cause nervousness, agitation, headache, rapid rise in blood pressure.	Safety not established below age 12 years. May interact with a variety of psychotropic and non-psychotropic drugs. Concurrent use of tricyclic drugs may lessen the effect of Clonidine. May enhance the central nervous system-depressive effects of certain drugs. May be preferred over stimulants for children with low IQ.

Figure 3.1 — Psychotropic Medications Used To Manage

Name and Type	Target Symptoms	Dosage
Name: Lithium Carbonate (Eskalith & Eskalith CR; Lithonate, Lithotabs) **Type:** Mood Stabilizer	Severe aggression, rage, violent outbursts	**Target range:** 300 to 2100 mg/day. Final dosage depends on serum level of drug. Monitor serum during treatment to check if therapeutic levels are being maintained. **Maximum:** Not specified. **Number of doses:** 2 per day. **Treatment response:** Development and maintenance of drug "steady state" required. Response usually apparent 3 to 6 weeks after start of treatment.
Name: Haloperidol (Haldol Decanoate) **Type:** Neuroleptic (tranquilizer)	Severe aggression, rage, violent outbursts	**Target range:** 0.04 to 0.21 mg/kg/day or 1 to 6 mg/day. **Maximum:** Not specified. **Number of doses:** 1 to 3 per day. **Treatment response:** Varies; usually within several weeks.
Name: Pimozide (Orap) **Type:** Neuroleptic (antidyskinetic)	Severe aggression, rage, violent outbursts	**Target range:** 5 to 6 mg/day (vs. 1 to 2 mg/day) **Maximum:** 0.3 mg/kg/day or 10 mg/day. **Number of doses:** 1 to 2 per day. **Treatment response:** Usually within several weeks.
Name: Carbamazepine (Tegretol) **Type:** Anticonvulsant	Severe aggression, rage, violent outbursts	**Target range:** 400 to 800 mg/day. Monitor for therapeutic levels. **Maximum:** 1000 mg/day. **Number of doses:** 3 per day. **Treatment response:** Within a few days to 2 weeks after the start of treatment.
Name: Propranolol Hydrochloride (Inderal or Inderide) **Type:** Beta-adrenergic blocker	Severe aggression, rage, violent outbursts	**Target range:** 50 to 960 mg/day. **Maximum:** 16 mg/kg/day or 300 mg/day. **Number of doses:** 2 to 3 per day. **Treatment response:** Generally within 5 weeks.

Notes

Most common side effects in bold. Table adapted from material in Greenhill, L. L. (1992). Pharmacologic treatment of Attention Deficit Hyperactivity Disorder. Psychiatric Clinics of North America, 15, 1-27; Wilens, T. E., & Biederman, J. (1992). The stimulants. Psychiatric Clinics of North America, 15, 191-222; Campbell, M., Gonzalez, N. M., & Silva, R. R. (1992). The pharmacologic treatment of conduct disorders and rage outbursts. Psychiatric Clinics of North America, 15, 69-85; Fetner, H. H., & Geller, B. (1992). Lithium and tricyclic antidepressants. Psychiatric Clinics of North America, 15, 223-241 (1992);

Conduct Disorder and Related Symptoms (Continued)

Common Side Effects	Special Concerns
Weight gain, stomach ache, headache, tremor. Variety of other possible side effects, including nausea, exacerbation of acne. Sedation and cognitive dulling less likely than with neuroleptics.	Safety not established below age 12 years. Use with caution with other psychotropics. Drugs that interfere with kidney function (e.g., nonsteroidal anti-inflammatory agents taken during menses), drugs that impact on hydration (e.g., diuretics, non-prescription diet systems), and illness may disrupt Lithium steady-state and lead to drug toxicity. Symptoms of toxicity include diarrhea, vomiting, drowsiness, muscular weakness, lack of coordination. Must have constant access to water during treatment.
Sedation, parkinsonian symptoms, acute dystonic reactions, weight gain, withdrawal and tardive dyskinesias. Numerous other side effects, including tics, akathisia, other tardive syndromes, seizures, dry skin, flushing, dilated pupils, dry mouth, increased heart rate, cardiac problems, respiratory problems, rash, photosensivity, change in hormonal functioning, jaundice, bone marrow problems, constipation, difficulty urinating, low blood pressure, cognitive impairment, dizziness, akathasia, akinesia, confusion, memory problems, vision problems, kidney and liver problems. Must discontinue drug treatment slowly. When discontinued, insomnia, nightmares, diarrhea, vomiting, behavioral rebound, and withdrawal or tardive dyskinesia possible.	Do not use with children under 3 years of age. Use cautiously if concurrently taking anticonvulsants and a variety of other drugs. Potentiates effects of central nervous system depressants (e.g., alcohol). Use cautiously if history of cardiovascular problems. Monitor involuntary movements continually.
Similar side effects to Haloperidol but tend to be less frequent and/or intense Mild sedation relative to Haloperidol.	Not recommended for children age 3 years and under. Use cautiously with other psychotropic drugs.
Drowsiness, poor coordination, skin rashes, leukopenia. Also blurred vision, dizziness, fatigue, blood problems, mild ataxia, mild dysarthria. Tardive dyskinesia and parkinsonian symptoms are not side effects. Has minimal impact on cognition.	Not recommended for children under age 6 years. Concurrent or recent treatment with a monoamine oxidase inhibitor contraindicated. Increases sensitivity to tricyclic drugs.
Bradycardia, hypertension. Also insomnia, fatigue, hallucinations, nausea, vomiting, bronchospasm, blood problems. Discontinue gradually.	Safety not established for children. Age limit not specified. Interacts with various other general and psychotropic medications. Should not be used concurrently with Haloperidol. Contraindicated if history of heat problems and/or asthma.

Notes Continued

Neuroleptics in pediatric psychiatry. <u>Psychiatric Clinics of North America</u>, <u>15</u>, 243-276; Details not listed in these articles obtained from Olin, B. R., Hebel, S. K., & Dewein, A. C. (Eds.) (January, 1995). <u>Drug facts and comparisons</u>. St Louis: Facts and Comparisons, Inc. For quick access to information on other side effects, warnings, and drug interactions, see Griffith, H. W. (1995). <u>Complete guide to prescription and nonprescription drugs, 1996 Edition</u>. New York: The Body Press/Perigee.

What is the Effectiveness of Medication Therapy?

Evidence exists that the medications listed on pages 64-67 offer a positive, short-term impact on a few of the conduct-disorder symptoms in some children. For example, 50 to 75 percent of children accurately diagnosed with ADHD benefit from stimulants through decreases in inattention, impulsivity, hyperactivity, non-compliance, and/or verbal and physical aggression.[186,190,191]

Problem symptoms usually do not respond equally well to the same stimulant dose, and children often respond differently to the same dosage level on different days.[192]

Lithium appears beneficial for the short-term treatment of severe aggression with a strong affective and episodic component, without significant side effects.[95,193] However, the few studies that have been done fail to clarify what percentage of patients respond well to Lithium.

neuroleptics—antipsychotic medications

The *neuroleptics* are beneficial for treating the severely aggressive behaviors of hospitalized children with conduct disorder diagnoses.[95,194] Many aggressive patients do respond to the neuroleptics but unfortunately, there are numerous, serious side effects associated with treatment. Because of these side effects, this class of drugs should be avoided until other options have been exhausted.

Since clinicians consider medication to be an adjunct, rather than an alternative, to the psychological therapies, there are no studies that explicitly contrast these two types of treatment for the conduct disorders. However, research conducted on children diagnosed with ADHD indicate that psychological therapies have, at best, equaled the effectiveness of medication therapy.[195] Studies of children diagnosed with ADHD that contrast medication-only, psychological therapy-only, and combined treatment groups, indicate that the combined treatment groups generally perform only slightly better than the medication-only groups.[159,196]

The likelihood of symptoms reappearing after discontinuing medication treatment is less if effective and sustainable environmental interventions are firmly in place.

Despite the short-term efficacy of these medications, there is currently no evidence that treatment with any medication cures the conduct disorders.[95,197] There is also no conclusive evidence that the stimulants cure the symptoms of ADHD.[190,197]

Figure 3.2 — Evidence for Short-Term and Long-Term Treatment Effectiveness

Treatment Program	Short-term Effectiveness	Long-term Effectiveness
Behavior Therapy		
Parent Training	Yes	Preliminary
School-Based Programs		
CLASS	Yes	Preliminary
RECESS	Yes	No
Treatment Foster Care	Yes	Preliminary
Cognitive Therapy		
Child Problem-Solving Skills Training	Yes	Preliminary
Family Therapy		
Functional Family Therapy	Yes	No
Multisystemic Treatment	Yes	Preliminary
Group Therapy		
Community-Center Based	Yes	No
Summer Treatment Program	No	No
Psychodynamic Approach		
Dyadic Skills Training	No	No
Medications	Yes	No

*Therapy Notes
from the Desk of
Pat Owen*

Mother and stepfather are monitoring and tracking
Shawn's behavior and activities at home and school.
The school-home report card seems to be working well.
Shawn's teachers report that he is more compliant and
that his grades are better. Skipping school does not
appear to be a current problem, and there have been
fewer fights and no behavior that requires police
intervention. For the next three months, recommend
monthly phone contact with parents, with face-to-face
booster sessions if needed. Mother is concerned about
Shawn's affect. He does display some mild symptoms
of depression/anxiety. Will continue to monitor. If
symptoms do not improve, will consider other psychosocial interventions, as well as medications.

Appendix: For the Clinician's Bookshelf— Recommended Resources

Research and Theory

Kazdin, A. E. (1985). <u>Treatment of antisocial behavior in children and adolescents</u>. Homewood, IL: Dorsey Press.

Loeber, R., & Farrington, D. P. (Eds.) (1998). <u>Serious and violent juvenile offenders: Risk factors and successful interventions</u>. Thousand Oaks, CA: Sage.

McCord, J. & Tremblay, R. E. (1992). <u>Preventing antisocial behavior: Interventions from birth to adolescence</u>. New York: Guilford Press.

Patterson, G. R., Reid, J. B., & Dishion, T. J. (1992). <u>Antisocial Boys</u>. Eugene, OR: Castalia Press.

Peplar, D. J., & Rubin, K. H. (1991). <u>The development and treatment of childhood aggression</u>. Hillsdale, NJ: Lawrence Erlbaum.

Stoff, D. M., Breiling, J., & Maser, J. D. (Eds.). (1997). <u>Handbook of antisocial behavior</u>. New York: John Wiley and Sons.

Assessment

Mash, E. J., & Terdal, L. G. (1997). <u>Assessment of childhood disorders</u>, 3rd Edition. New York: Guilford Press.

O'Neil, R. E., Horner, R. H., Albin, R. W., Storey, K., & Sprague, J. R. (1990). <u>Functional analysis of problem behavior: A practical assessment guide</u>. Sycamore, IL: Sycamore.

Salvia, J., & Ysseldyck, J. E. (1991). <u>Assessment</u>. Boston: Houghton Mifflin.

Environmentally-based Treatments

Parent Training: For clinicians

Blechman, E. A. (1985). <u>Solving child behavior problems: At home and at school</u>. Champaign, IL: Research Press.

Dishion, T. J., Kavanagh, K., & Soberman, L. (In press). <u>Adolescent Transitions Program: Assessment and intervention sourcebook</u>. New York: Guilford Press.

Forehand, R., & McMahon, R. J. (1981). <u>Helping the noncompliant child: A clinician's guide to parent training</u>. New York: Guilford Press.

Patterson, G. R., Reid, J. B., Jones, R. R., & Conger, R. E. (1975). <u>Families with aggressive children</u>. Eugene, OR: Castalia Press.

Ramsey, E., Beland, K., and Miller, T. (1995). <u>Second Step: Parenting strategies for a safer tomorrow.</u> Seattle, WA: Committee for Children.

Sanders, M. R., & Dadds, M. R. (1993). <u>Behavioral family intervention</u>. Boston: Allyn and Bacon.

Webster-Stratton, C. & Herbert, M. (1994). <u>Troubled families, problem children - Working with parents: A collaborative process.</u>. Chichester, England: John Wiley & Sons.

Parent Training: For Parents

Dishion, T. J., & Patterson, G. R. (1995). <u>Preventive parenting with love, encouragement, and limits: The preschool years.</u> Eugene, OR: Castalia Press.

Forgatch, M. S., & Patterson, G. R. (1987). <u>Parents and adolescents living together — Part 2: Family problem solving</u>. Eugene, OR: Castalia Press.

Patterson, G. R. (1976). <u>Living with children: New methods for parents and teachers (revised)</u>. Champaign, IL: Research Press.

Patterson, G. R. (1977). <u>Families: Applications of social learning to family life. (revised)</u>. Champaign, IL: Research Press.

Patterson, G. R., & Forgatch, M. S. (1987). <u>Parents and adolescents living together — Part 1: The basics</u>. Eugene, OR: Castalia Press.

Webster-Stratton, C. (1997). <u>The incredible years: A trouble-shooting guide for parents of children aged 3-8</u>. Toronto, Ontario: Umbrella Press.

School Interventions

Walker, H. M. (1995). <u>The acting-out child: Coping with classroom disruption (revised)</u>. Longmont, CO: Sopris West, Inc.

Walker, H. M., Colvin, G., & Ramsey, E. (1995). <u>Antisocial behavior in school: Strategies and best practices</u>. Pacific Grove, CA: Brooks/Cole.

Treatment Foster Care

Chamberlain, P. (1994). <u>Family connections: A Treatment Foster Care model for adolescents with delinquency</u>. Eugene, OR: Castalia Publishing.

Chamberlain, P. (1998). <u>Blueprints for violence prevention, book eight: Treatment Foster Care</u>. Boulder, CO: Center for the Study and Prevention of Violence.

Cognitive Therapy

Greenberg, M. T., Kusché, C. & Mihalic, S. F. (1998). <u>Blueprints for violence prevention, book ten: Promoting Alternative Thinking Strategies (PATHS)</u>. Boulder, CO: Center for the Study and Prevention of Violence.

Kendall, P. C., & Braswell, L. (1985). <u>Cognitive-behavioral therapy for impulsive children</u>. New York: Guilford Press.

Camp, B. W., & Bash, M. A. S. (1985). <u>Think aloud: Increasing social and cognitive skills — A problem solving program for children</u>. Champaign, IL: Research Press.

Family Therapy

Alexander, J. F., & Parsons, B. (1982). <u>Functional Family Therapy</u>. Monterey, CA: Brooks/Cole.

Alexander, J., Barton, C., Gordon, D., Grotpeter, J., Hansson, K., Harrison, R., Mears, S., Mihalic, S., Parsons, B., Pugh, C., Schulman, S., Waldron, H., & Sexton, T. (1998). <u>Blueprints for violence prevention, book three: Functional Family Therapy</u>. Boulder, CO: Center for the Study and Prevention of Violence.

Henggeler, S. W. (1990). <u>Family therapy and beyond: A multisystemic approach to treating the behavior problems of children and adolescents</u>. Pacific Grove, CA: Brooks/Cole.

Henggeler, S. W., Mihalic, S. F., Rone, L., Thomas, C., & Timmons-Mitchell, J. (1998). <u>Blueprints for violence prevention, book six: Multisystemic Therapy</u>. Boulder, CO: Center for the Study and Prevention of Violence.

Robin, A. L., & Foster, S. L. (1989). <u>Negotiating parent-adolescent conflict: A behavioral-family systems approach</u>. New York: Guilford Press.

Group Therapy

Feldman, R. A., Caplinger, T. E., & Wodarski, J. S. (1983). <u>The St. Louis Conundrum: The effective treatment of antisocial youths</u>. Englewood Cliffs, NJ: Prentice Hall.

Pelham, W. E. (1995). <u>Children's Summer Day Treatment Program manual</u>. Unpublished manual. Pittsburgh: ADD Program, Western Psychiatric Institute and Clinic, University of Pittsburgh School of Medicine.

Psychodynamic Therapy

Belsky, J., & Nezworski, T. (Eds.) (1988). <u>Clinical implications of attachment</u>. Hillsdale, NJ: Lawrence Erlbaum.

Greenberg, M. T., Cicchetti, D., & Cummings, E. M. (Eds.) (1990). <u>Attachment in the preschool years: Theory, research, and intervention</u>. Chicago: University of Chicago Press.

Treatment for Co-occurring Problems

Barkley, R. A. (1990). <u>Attention Deficit Hyperactivity Disorder: A handbook for diagnosis and treatment</u>. New York: Guilford Press.

Baucom, D., & Epstein, N. (1990). <u>Cognitive-behavioral marital therapy</u>. New York: Brunner/Mazel.

Biological Treatments

Ammerman, R. T. & Hersen, M. (Eds.) (1986), <u>Pharmacological and behavioral treatment: An integrative approach</u>. New York: John Wiley and Sons.

Internet Resources

World Wide Web. For information about parenting and the conduct disorders as well as links to other Web sites relevant to the treatment of the conduct disorders, visit the Oregon Social Learning Center homepage (http://www.oslc.org).

Psychological and Medical Literature Databases. Many university and medical center libraries now have on-line access to abstract databases such as PsychInfo and Medline. Contact an academic library in your state for further information.

Other Resources

Up-to-date information about the treatment and the prevention of the conduct disorders is disseminated through various federal agencies such as the U.S. Department of Education (DOE), the U.S. Office of Juvenile Justice and Delinquency Prevention (OJJDP), the National Institute of Mental Health (NIMH), the National Institute of Drug Abuse (NIDA), the National Institute of Alcohol Abuse and the Addictions (NIAAA), advocacy groups such as the National Mental Health Association (NMHA), and through professional organizations such as the Society for Prevention Research (SPR), and the American Psychological Association (APA). Contact your local library for addresses, or search the World Wide Web for on-line information. Many such Web sites can be accessed via the Oregon Local Learning Center homepage (http://www.oslc.org).

Glossary

A

across-time correlations—*the extent to which a person's test scores remain in a similar rank compared to others across time. For example, if a test is highly stable, Suzy will score high on three separate testings, Sam moderate, and Jean low.*

amygdala—*a brain structure that plays a role in emotional behavior such as aggression, motivation, and memory functions*

B

baseline—*a period of time prior to the beginning of a therapeutic intervention*

behavioral rebound—*an exaggeration of the presenting complaints five to 15 hours after the last dose of stimulants*

C

case manager—*a person, typically a social worker, who oversees all aspects of the client's treatment program*

clinically significant—*a pattern of behavioral or psychological symptoms that has become established enough, severe enough, and impairing enough to interfere with a child's day-to-day functioning in one or more settings (i.e., home, school, community)*

conscious—*in the person's awareness*

contingency contract—*a plan for the positive and negative consequences that follow specific child behaviors*

contingency management program—*a system for rewarding good behaviors and providing costs for misbehaviors*

correlates—*the degree to which two scores are systematically related to each other "co-relate"*

D

deviant peer groups—*friendship groups comprising children who have difficulty with failing grades, engage in illegal activities, have little contact with prosocial activities, have parents who provide little structure or monitoring*

developmental history—*significant events and milestones during childhood such as age the child first walked, talked, etc.*

double bind messages—*two opposite messages are conveyed simultaneously, so the actual message is unclear. For example, a person says "everything is fine" in a hostile, anxious voice*

dysfunctional—*patterns of behavior that have distressing and problematic outcomes*

E

encoding—*the registering of information in the brain*

F

face valid—*the content of test items directly assesses a self-evident psychological construct*

G

generalization — *occurrence of the relevant behavior under non-training conditions*

H

homeostasis—*equilibrium or balance*

hypothalamus—*a brain structure involved in the control of body temperature, heart rate, blood pressure, etc.*

I

internal reliability—*the extent to which the various items on a test are related to one another*

inter-observer reliability—*degree of agreement among the ratings of various observers*

inter-parental reliability—*the degree of agreement on test scores between parents*

interpretation—*the meaning or beliefs that a person holds about an event*

M

mental disorder—*a clinically significant pattern of behavioral or psychological symptoms associated with one or more major negative outcomes (i.e., distress, pain, injury, disability, confinement)*

modeling—*demonstrating*

monitoring—*hour-to-hour each day, parent knows who their child is with, where their child is, and what their child is doing*

multimodal—*several different psychological therapies combined with medications*

N

negative reinforcement—*the discontinuation of an undesired event (e.g., parents fighting) following a behavior (e.g., child hits sibling) rewards the occurrence of that behavior (i.e., the hit)*

neuroleptics—*antipsychotic medications*

neurotransmitters—*chemical agents that carry information between nerve cells in the body and affect behavior, mood, and thoughts*

P

pathological—a disruption in "normal" functioning

positive reinforcement—the delivery of a desired event (e.g., parent says, "Great job, Joe!" and gives Joe a hug) following a behavior (e.g., child playing nicely with sibling) which results in an increase of that behavior

prosocial—responsible, socially considerate behavior

psychosocial—history of significant social developments such as family interactions, behavior in friendships, adjustment at school

psychotropic—broadly, a substance that impacts on the behavior, emotions, or thoughts of an individual

R

rate-per-minute—the average number of specific behaviors of interest occurring in one minute

recidivism—relapse rate (e.g., getting arrested again)

relational aggression—harm perpetrated against others using indirect, non-physical means such as manipulation, threats, and exclusion

respite care—short-term (e.g., a weekend) out-of-home placements

reuptake—reabsorption of a neurotransmitter into the cell that released it

S

stability—the extent to which a child or adolescent retains their standing relative to other individuals on a psychological construct across time

stimulant—a medication that increases the arousal of the Central Nervous System

synapse—the space between individual nerve cells in the brain

T

test-retest reliability—the extent to which those tested obtain similar scores relative to each other on each administration of the test

titration—slow increase in medication until significant effects on the problem behaviors are noticed

token economy system—for specific behaviors, a child earns points or other currency that can be traded in for specific rewards

tolerance—diminished responsiveness to a drug due to repeated use, thus requiring larger doses to have the same effect

V

validity—the extent to which the test measures what it claims to measure

W

wandering—child spends time in unstructured, adult-unsupervised settings

Bibliography

1. Robins, L. N. (1981). Epidemiological approaches to natural history research: Antisocial disorders in children. Journal of the American Academy of Child Psychiatry, 20, 566-580.

2. Kazdin, A. E. (1994). Interventions for aggressive and antisocial children. In L. D. Eron, J. H. Gentry, & P. Schlegel (Eds.), Reason to hope: A psychological perspective on violence and youth (pp. 341-382). Washington, DC: American Psychological Association.

3. Eddy, J. M., & Swanson-Garbskov (1997). Juvenile justice and delinquency prevention in the United States: The influence of theories and traditions on policies and practices. In T. P. Gullota, G. R. Adams, & R. Montemayor (Eds.), Delinquent Violent Youth (pp. 12-52). Thousand Oaks, CA: Sage

4. Wolff, S. (1961). Symptomatology and outcome of preschool children with behavior disorders attending a child guidance clinic. Journal of Child Psychology and Psychiatry, 2, 269-276.

5. American Psychiatric Association (1994). Diagnostic and Statistical Manual of Mental Disorders, Fourth Edition. Washington, DC, American Psychiatric Association.

6. Offord, D. R., Boyle, M. C., & Racine, Y. A. (1991). The epidemiology of antisocial behavior in childhood and adolescence. In D. J. Peplar, & K. H. Rubin (Eds.), The development and treatment of childhood aggression (pp. 31-54). Hillsdale, NJ: Lawrence Erlbaum Associates.

7. Rutter, M., Cox, A., Tupling, C., Berger, M., & Yule, W. (1975). Attainment and adjustment in two geographical areas. I. The prevalence of psychiatric disorder. British Journal of Psychiatry, 126, 493-509.

8. McGee, R., Feehan, M., Williams, S., & Anderson, J. (1992). DSM-III disorders from age 11 to age 15 years. Journal of the American Academy of Child and Adolescent Psychiatry, 31, 50-59.

9. Cohen, P. (1993). An epidemiological study of disorders in late childhood and adolescence: I. Age- and gender-specific prevalence. Journal of Child Psychology and Psychiatry and Allied Disciplines, 34, 851-867.

10. McGee, R., Feehan, M., Williams, S., & Partridge, R. (1990). DSM-III disorders in a large sample of adolescents. Journal of the American Academy of Child and Adolescent Psychiatry, 29, 611-619.

11. Rutter, M. (1981). The city and the child. American Journal of Orthopsychiatry, 51, 610-625.

12. Patterson, G. R., Reid, J. B., & Dishion, T. J. (1992). Antisocial boys. Eugene, OR: Castalia Publishing.

13. Loeber, R., & Dishion, T. J. (1983). Early predictors of male delinquency: A review. Psychological Bulletin, 94, 68-99.

14. Lipsey, M. W., & Derzon, J. H. (1999). Predictors of violent or serious delinquency in adolescence and early adulthood: A synthesis of longitudinal research. In R. Loeber & D.P. Farrington (Eds), Serious and Violent Juvenile Offenders (pp.86-105). Thousand Oaks, CA: Sage

15. Olweus, D. (1979). Stability of aggressive reaction patterns in males: A review. Psychological Bulletin, 86, 852-875.

16. Farrington, D. P. (1987). Early precursors of frequent offending. In J. Q. Wilson & G. C. Loury (Eds.), From children to citizens, vol. 3: Families, schools, and delinquency prevention (pp. 27-50). New York: Springer-Verlag.

17. Robins, L. N. (1966). Deviant children grown up: A sociological and psychiatric study of sociopathic personality. Baltimore: Williams and Wilkins.

18. Rutter, M., & Giller, H. (1983). Juvenile delinquency: Trends and perspectives. New York: Penguin Books.

19. Loeber, R. (1982). The stability of antisocial and delinquent behavior: A review. Child Development, 53, 1431-1446.

20. Loeber, R. (1990). Development and risk factors of juvenile antisocial behavior and delinquency. Clinical Psychology Review, 10, 1-41.

21. Kazdin, A. E. (1987). Conduct disorder in childhood and adolescence. Newbury Park, CA: Sage.

22. Offord, D. R., Sullivan, K., Allen, N., & Abrams, N. (1979). Delinquency and hyperactivity. Journal of Nervous and Mental Disorders, 167, 734-741.

23. LeBlanc, M., & Frechette, M. (1989). Male offending from latency to adulthood. New York: Springer-Verlag.

24. Patterson, G. R., & Capaldi, D. C. (1994). <u>Frequency of offending and violent behavior.</u> Unpublished manuscript. Eugene, OR: Oregon Social Learning Center.

25. Loeber, R. (1988). Natural histories of conduct problems, delinquency, and associated substance use: Evidence for developmental progressions. In B. B. Lahey & A. E. Kasdin (Eds.), <u>Advances in clinical child psychopathology, 11</u>, (pp. 73-124). New York: Plenum.

26. Patterson, G. R., DeBaryshe, B. D., & Ramsey, E. A. (1989). A developmental perspective on antisocial behavior. <u>American Psychologist, 44</u>, 329-335.

27. Robins, L. N. (1991). Conduct disorder. <u>Journal of Child Psychology and Psychiatry, 20</u>, 566-680.

28. Robins, L. N. (1970). The adult development of the antisocial child. <u>Seminars in Psychiatry, 6</u>, 420-434.

29. Robins, L. N., & Ratcliff, K. S. (1978-1979). Risk factors in the continuation of childhood antisocial behaviors into adulthood. <u>International Journal of Mental Health, 7</u>, 96-116.

30. Farrington, D. P. (1983). Offending from 10 to 25 years of age. In K. T. Van Dusen, & S. A. Mednick (Eds.), <u>Prospective studies of crime and delinquency</u> (pp. 17-37). Boston: Kluwer-Nijhoff.

31. Robins, L. N. (1978). Sturdy childhood predictors of adult antisocial behavior: Replications from longitudinal studies. <u>Psychological Medicine, 8</u>, 611-622.

32. Eron, L. D., Huesmann, L. R., & Zelli, A. (1991). The role of parental variables in the learning of aggression. In D. J. Peplar, & K. H. Rubin (Eds.), <u>The development and treatment of childhood aggression</u> (pp. 169-188). Hillsdale, NJ: Lawrence Erlbaum Associates.

33. Farrington, D. P. (1991). Childhood aggression and adult violence: Early precursors and later life outcomes. In D. J. Peplar, & K. H. Rubin (Eds.), <u>The development and treatment of childhood aggression</u> (pp. 5-29). Hillsdale, NJ: Lawrence Erlbaum Associates.

34. Serbin, L. A., Moskowitz, D. S., Schwartzman, A. E., & Ledingham, J. E. (1991). Aggressive, withdrawn, and aggressive/withdrawn children in adolescence: Into the next generation. In D. J. Peplar, & K. H. Rubin (Eds.), <u>The development and treatment of childhood aggression</u> (pp. 55-70). Hillsdale, NJ: Erlbaum.

35. Huesmann, L. R. , Eron, L. D., Lefkowitz, M. M., & Walder, L. O. (1984). The stability of aggression over time and generations. <u>Developmental Psychology, 20</u>, 1120-1134.

36. Crick, N. R., & Grotpeter, J. K. (1995). Relational aggression, gender, and social-psychological adjustment. <u>Child Development, 66</u>, 710-722.

37. Stoolmiller, M. S. (1994). Antisocial behavior, delinquent peer association, and unsupervised wandering for boys: Growth and change from childhood to early adolescence. <u>Multivariate Behavioral Research, 29</u>, 263-288.

38. Wilson, H. (1980). Parental supervision: A neglected aspect of delinquency. <u>British Journal of Criminology, 20</u>, 203-254.

39. Fesbach, S. (1970). Sex differences in children's modes of aggressive responses toward outsiders. <u>Merrill-Palmer Quarterly, 15</u>, 249-258.

40. Patterson, G. R., Capaldi, D., & Bank, L. (1991). An early starter model for predicting delinquency. In D. J. Peplar & K. H. Rubin (Eds.), <u>The development and treatment of childhood aggression</u> (pp. 139-168). Hillsdale, NJ: Lawrence Erlbaum Associates.

41. Patterson, G. R., Yoerger, K., & Stoolmiller, M. S. (in press). A developmental model for late-onset delinquency. In D. Stoff, J. Maser, & J. Breiling (Eds.), <u>Handbook of antisocial behavior.</u> New York: John Wiley & Sons.

42. Costello, E. J., Edelbrock, C. S., Costello, A. J., Dulcan, M. K., Burns, B. J., & Brent, D. (1988). Psychopathology in pediatric primary care: The new hidden morbidity. <u>Pediatrics, 82</u>, 415-424.

43. Sleater, E. K., & Ullmann, R. L. (1981). Can the physician diagnose hyperactivity in the office? <u>Pediatrics, 67</u>, 13-17.

44. Patterson, G. R., Duncan, T. E., Reid, J. B., & Bank, L. (1994). <u>Systematic maternal errors in predicting son's future arrests.</u> Unpublished manuscript, Oregon Social Learning Center, Eugene.

45. Reid, J. B., Kavanagh, K., & Baldwin, D. V. (1987). Abusive parents' perceptions of child problem behaviors: An example of parental bias. <u>Journal of Abnormal Child Psychology, 15</u>, 457-466.

46. Lorber, T. (1981). <u>Parental tracking of childhood behavior as a function of family stress</u>. Unpublished doctoral dissertation, University of Oregon, Eugene.

47. Holleran, P. A., Littman, D. C., Freund, R., Schmaling, K., & Heeren, J. (1982). A signal detection approach to social perception: Identification of negative and positive behaviors by parents of normal and distressed children. <u>Journal of Abnormal Child Psychology, 10</u>, 547-557.

48. Barkley, R. A. (1990). <u>Attention Deficit Hyperactivity Disorder: A handbook for diagnosis and treatment</u>. New York: Guilford Press.

49. Patterson, G. R., Reid, J. B., Jones, R. R., & Conger, R. E. (1975). <u>A social learning approach to family intervention, vol. 1: Families with aggressive children</u>. Eugene, OR: Castalia Publishing.

50. Achenbach, T. M. (1991). <u>Manual for the Child Behavior Checklist/4-18 and 1991 profile</u>. Burlington, VT: University of Vermont Department of Psychiatry.

51. Pelham, W. E., Gnagy, E. M., Greenslade, K. E., & Milich, R. (1992). Teacher ratings of DSM-III-R symptoms for the disruptive behavior disorders. <u>Journal of the American Academy of Child and Adolescent Psychiatry, 31</u>, 210-218.

52. Achenbach, T. M. (1991). <u>Manual for the Teacher's Report Form and 1991 profile</u>. Burlington, VT: University of Vermont Department of Psychiatry.

53. Achenbach, T. M. (1991). <u>Manual for the Youth Self-Report and 1991 profile</u>. Burlington, VT: University of Vermont Department of Psychiatry.

54. Sandberg, D. E., Meyer-Bahlburg, H. F. L., & Yager, T. J. (1991). The Child Behavior Checklist nonclinical standardization samples: Should they be utilized as norms? <u>Journal of the American Academy of Child and Adolescent Psychiatry, 30</u>, 124-134.

55. Achenbach, T. M., Bird, H. R., Canino, G., & Phares, V. (1990). Epidemiological comparisons of Puerto Rico and U. S. mainland children: Parent, teacher, and self-reports. <u>Journal of the American Academy of Child and Adolescent Psychiatry, 29</u>, 84-93.

56. Pelham, W. E., Evans, S. W., Gnagy, E. M., & Greenslade, K. E. (1992). Teacher ratings of DSM-III-R symptoms for the disruptive behavior disorders: Prevalence, factor analyses, and conditional probabilities in a special education sample. <u>School Psychology Review, 21</u>, 285-299.

57. Kovacs, M. (1980). Ratings scales to assess depression in school aged children. <u>Acta Paedopsychiatrica, 46</u>, 305-315.

58. Woodcock, R. W. (1977). <u>Woodcock-Johnson Psycho-Educational Battery: Technical report</u>. Allen, TX: DLM Teaching Resources.

59. Schaffer, D., Fisher, P., Dulcan, M., Davies, M., Piacentini, J., Schwab-Stone, M., Lahey, B., Bourdon, K., Jensen, P., Bird, H., Canino, G., & Regier, D. (1995). <u>The NIMH Diagnostic Interview Schedule for Children (DISC 2.3): Description, acceptability, prevalences, and performance in the MECA study</u>. Unpublished manuscript, New York State Psychiatric Institute, New York.

60. Costello, A. J., Edelbrock, C., Dulcan, M. K., Kalas, R., & Klaric, S. H. (1984). <u>Development and testing of the NIMH Diagnostic Interview Schedule for Children in a clinic population</u>. Final report (Contract No. RFP-DB-81-0027). Rockville, MD: Center for Epidemiologic Studies, National Institutes of Mental Health.

61. Weschler, D. (1991). <u>The Wechsler Intelligence Scale for Children —Third edition</u>. New York: The Psychological Corporation.

62. Fisher, P., Shaffer, D., Wicks, J., & Piacentini, J. (1989). <u>A users' manual for the DISC-2 (Diagnostic Interview Schedule for Children, Version 2)</u>. Unpublished manual, New York State Psychiatric Institute, New York, NY.

63. Piacentini, J., Shaffer, D., Fisher, P., Schwab-Stone, M., Davies, M., & Gioia, P. (1993). The Diagnostic Interview Schedule for Children — Revised (DISC-R): III. Concurrent criterion validity. <u>Journal of the American Academy of Child and Adolescent Psychiatry, 32</u>, 658-665.

64. Edelbrock, C., & Costello, A. J. (1988). Structured psychiatric interviews for children. In M. Rutter, A. H. Tuma, & I. S. Lann (Eds.), <u>Assessment and diagnosis in child psychopathology</u> (pp. 87-112). New York: Guilford Press.

65. Edelbrock, C., Costello, A. J., Dulcan, M. K., Conover, N .C., & Kalas, R. (1986). Parent-child agreement on child psychiatric symptoms assessed via structured interview. Journal of Child Psychology and Psychiatry, 27, 181-190.

66. Costello, E. J., Edelbrock, C., & Costello, A. J. (1985). The validity of the NIMH Diagnostic Interview Schedule for Children: A comparison between pediatric and psychiatric referrals. Journal of Abnormal Child Psychology, 13, 579-595.

67. Exner, J. E. (1993). The Rorschach: A comprehensive system: Volume I: Basic foundations. Somerset, NJ: John Wiley & Sons.

68. Hathaway, S. R., Butcher, J. N., & McKinley, J. C. (1989). Minnesota Multiphasic Personality Inventory - 2. Minneapolis: University of Minnesota Press.

69. Chamberlain, P., & Reid, J. B. (1987). Parent observation and report of child symptoms. Behavioral Assessment, 2, 97-109.

70. Kraemer, H. C., & Thiemann, S. (1989). A strategy to use soft data effectively in randomized controlled clinical trails. Journal of Consulting and Clinical Psychology, 57 (1), 148-154.

71. Eddy, J. M., Stoolmiller, M. S., Reid, J. B., Dishion, T. J., & Bank, L. (1995, November). A method for the development of reliable measures of change. Paper presented at the 29th annual convention of the Association for the Advancement of Behavior Therapy, Washington, DC.

72. Chamberlain, P. (1994). Family connections: A treatment foster care model for adolescents with delinquency. Eugene, OR: Castalia Publishing.

73. Sanders, M. R., & Dadds, M. R. (1993). Behavioral family intervention. Boston: Allyn & Bacon.

74. McMahon, R. J., & Forehand, R. (1988). Conduct Disorders. In E. J. Mash & L. G. Terdal (Eds.), Behavioral assessment of childhood disorders (pp. 105-156). New York: Guilford Press.

75. Robin, A. L., & Foster, S. L. (1989). Negotiating parent-adolescent conflict: A behavioral-family systems approach. New York: Guilford Press.

76. McConaughy, S. H., & Achenbach, T. M. (1988). Practical guide for the Child Behavior Checklist and related materials. Burlington, VT: University of Vermont, Department of Psychiatry.

77. Sattler, J. M. (1990). Assessment of children, (Third edition). San Diego: Jerome Sattler.

78. Patterson, G. R., & Bank, L. (1986). Bootstrapping your way in the nomological thicket. Behavioral Assessment, 8, 49-73.

79. McConaughy, S. H., Achenbach, T. M., & Gent, C. L. (1988). Multiaxial empirically-based assessment: Parent, teacher, observational, cognitive, and personality correlates of Child Behavior Profiles for 6-11 year-old boys. Journal of Abnormal Child Psychology, 16, 485-509.

80. Weinrott, M. R., Reid, J. B., Bauske, R. W., & Brummet, B. (1981). Supplementing naturalistic observations with observer impressions. Behavioral Assessment, 3, 151-159.

81. Horne, A. M., & Sayger, T. V. (1990). Treating conduct and oppositional defiant disorders in children. New York: Pergammon Press.

82. Dunford, F. W., & Elliot, D. S. (1982). Identifying career offenders with self-report data (Grant No. MH27552). Washington, DC: National Institute of Mental Health.

83. Anderson, J. C., Williams, S. M., McGee, R., & Silva, P. A. (1987). DSM-III disorders in preadolescent children: Prevalence in a large sample from the general population. Archives of General Psychiatry, 44, 69-76.

84. Feldman, R. A., Caplinger, T. E., & Wodarski, J. S. (1983). The St. Louis conundrum: The effective treatment of antisocial youths. Englewood Cliffs, NJ: Prentice Hall.

85. Williams, J. R., & Gold, M. (1972). From delinquent behavior to official delinquency. Social Problems, 20, 209-229.

86. O'Neil, R. E., Horner, R. H., Albin, R. W., Storey, K., & Sprague, J. R. (1990). Functional analysis of problem behavior: A practical assessment guide. Sycamore, IL: Sycamore.

87. Lewinsohn, P. M., Hops, H., Roberts, R. E., Seeley, J. R., &Andrews, J. A. (1993). Adolescent psychopathology. I. Prevalence and incidence of depression and other DMS-III-R disorders in high school students. Journal of Abnormal Psychology, 102, 133-144.

88. McConaughy, S., H. (1993, February). <u>Comorbidity of DSM disorders and empirically derived syndromes in general population and clinically referred samples</u>. Paper presented at the fifth annual meeting of the Society for Research in Child and Adolescent Psychopathology, Santa Fe, NM.

89. Loney, J., & Milich, R. (1982). Hyperactivity, inattention, and aggression in clinical practice. In D. Routh & M. Wolraich (Eds.), <u>Advances in developmental and behavioral pediatrics</u> (Vol. 3, pp. 113-147). Greenwich, CT: JAI Press.

90. Hinshaw, S. P. (1987). On the distinction between attentional deficits/hyperactivity and conduct problems/aggression in child psychopathology. <u>Psychological Bulletin, 101</u>, 443-463.

91. Kazdin, A. E. (1988). <u>Child psychotherapy: Developing and identifying effective treatments</u>. New York: Pergammon Press.

92. Schaefer, C. E., & Millman, H. L. (Eds.) (1977). <u>Therapies for children</u>. San Francisco: Jossey Bass.

93. Kazdin, A. E. (1997). Practitioner reviews: Psychosocial ties for conduct disorder in children, <u>Journal of Child Psychology & Psychiatry and Allied Disciplines</u> 38(2), 161-178.

94. Brestan, E. V. & Eyberg, S. M. (1998). Effective psychosocial ties of conduct disorder in children and adolescents: 29 years, 82 studies, 5272 kids. <u>Journal of Clinical Child Psychology, 27</u>(2), 180-189.

95. Campbell, M., Gonzalez, N. M., & Silva, R. R. (1992). The pharmacologic treatment of conduct disorders and rage outbursts. <u>Psychiatric Clinics of North America, 15</u>, 69-85.

96. Dodge, K. (1980). Social cognition and children's aggressive behavior. <u>Child Development, 51</u>, 162-170.

97. Patterson, G. R. (1982). <u>Coercive family process</u>. Eugene, OR: Castalia Publishing.

98. McMahon, R. J., & Wells, K. C. (1989). Conduct disorders. In E. J. Mash & R. A. Barkley (Eds.), <u>Treatment of childhood disorders</u> (pp. 73-134). New York: Guilford Press.

99. Bank, L., Marlowe, J. H., Reid, J. B., Patterson, G. R., & Weinrott, M. R. (1991). A comparative evaluation of parent training interventions for families of chronic delinquents. <u>Journal of Abnormal Child Psychology, 19</u>, 15-33.

100. Greenberg, M. T., & Speltz, M. L. (1988). Attachment and the ontogeny of conduct problems. In J. Belsky & T. Nezworski (Eds.), <u>Clinical implications of attachment</u> (pp. 177-218). Hillsdale, NJ: Lawrence Erlbaum Associates.

101. Tolman, A. (1995). <u>Major depressive disorder: The latest assessment and treatment strategies</u>. Kansas City, MO: Compact Clinicals.

102. Brestan, E. V., & Eyber, S.M. (1998). Effective psychosocial treatments of conduct-disordered children and adolescents: 29 years, 82 studies, and 5,272 kids. <u>Journal of Clinical Child Psychology</u>, 27(2), 180-189.

103. Webster-Stratton, C., & Hammond, M. (1997). Treating children with early-onset conduct problems: A comparison of child and parent training interventions. <u>Journal of Consulting & Clinical Psychology, 65</u>(1), 93-109.

104. Webster-Stratton, C. (1998). Parent training with low-income families: Promoting parental engagement through a collaborative approach. In J. R. Lutzker (Ed.), <u>Handbook of child abuse research and treatment, Issues in clinical child psychology</u> (pp. 183-210). New York: Plenum Press.

105. Webster-Stratton, C. (1998). Preventing conduct problems in Head Start children: Strengthening parenting competencies. <u>Journal of Consulting & Clinical Psychology, 66</u>(5), 715-730.

106. Webster-Stratton, C., & Hancock, L. (1998). Training for parents of young children with conduct problems: Content, methods, and therapeutic processes. In J. M. Briesmeister & C. E. Schaefer (Eds.), <u>Handbook of parent training: Parents as co-therapists for children's behavior problems</u> (2nd ed., pp. 98-152). New York: John Wiley & Sons, Inc.

107. Patterson, G. R., Chamberlain, P., & Reid, J. B. (1982). A comparative evaluation of a parent training program. <u>Behavior Therapy, 13</u>, 638-650.

108. Miller, G. E., & Prinz, R. J. (1990). The enhancement of social learning family interventions for childhood conduct disorder. <u>Psychological Bulletin, 108</u>, 291-307.

109. Griest, D. L., & Wells, K. C. (1983). Behavioral family therapy with conduct disorders in children. <u>Behavior Therapy, 14</u>, 37-53.

110. Webster-Stratton, C. , Hollingsworth, T., & Kolpacoff, M. (1989). The long-term effectiveness of treatment and clinical significance of three cost-effective training programs for families with conduct problem children. Journal of Consulting and Clinical Psychology, 57, 550-553.

111. Baum, C. G., & Forehand, R. (1981). Long-term follow-up assessment of parent training by use of multiple-outcome measures. Behavior Therapy, 12, 643-652.

112. Patterson, G. R., & Fleischman, M. J. (1979). Maintenance of treatment effects: Some considerations concerning family systems and follow-up data. Behavior Therapy, 10, 168-185.

113. Walker, H. M., Colvin, G., & Ramsey, E. (1995). Antisocial behavior in school: Strategies and best practices. Pacific Grove, CA: Brooks/Cole.

114. Hops, H., & Walker, H. M. (1988). CLASS: Contingencies for Learning Academic and Social Skills. Seattle, WA: Educational Achievement Systems.

115. Walker, H., Hops, H., & Greenwood, C. (1993). RECESS: A program for reducing negative-aggressive behavior. Seattle, WA: Educational Achievement Systems.

116. Hops, H., Walker, H. M., Fleischman, D., Nagoshi, J., Omura, R., Skinrud, K., & Taylor, J. (1978). CLASS: A standardized in-class program for acting-out children. II. Field test evaluations. Journal of Educational Psychology, 70, 636-644.

117. Chamberlain, P., & Reid, J. B. (1998). Comparison of two community alternatives to incarceration for chronic juvenile offenders. Journal of Consulting and Clinical Psychology, 66(4), 624-633.

118. Eddy, J. M., & Chamberlain, P. (in press). Family management and deviant peer association as mediators of the impact of treatment condition on youth antisocial behavior. Journal of Consulting and Clinical Psychology.

119. Meyers, A. W., & Craighead, W. E. (Eds.) (1984). Cognitive behavior therapy with children. New York: Plenum.

120. Dodge, K. A., Pettit, G. S., McClaskey, C. L., & Brown, M. M. (1986). Social competence in children. Monographs of the Society for Research in Child Development, 51 (2, Serial No. 213).

121. Dodge, K. A. (1991). The structure and function of proactive and reactive aggression. In D. J. Peplar, & K. H. Rubin (Eds.), The development and treatment of childhood aggression (pp. 201-218). Hillsdale, NJ: Lawrence Erlbaum Associates.

122. Camp, B. W., & Bash, M. A. S. (1985). Think aloud: Increasing social and cognitive skills — A problem solving program for children. Champaign, IL: Research Press.

123. Spivak, G., Platt, J. J., & Shure, M. B. (1976). The problem-solving approach to adjustment. San Francisco: Jossey-Bass.

124. Peplar, D. J., King, G., & Byrd, W. (1991). A social-cognitively based social skills training program for aggressive children. In D. J. Peplar & K. H. Rubin (Eds.), The development and treatment of childhood aggression (pp. 361-386). Hillsdale, NJ: Lawrence Erlbaum Associates.

125. Guevermont, D. (1990). Social skills and peer relationship training. In R. A. Barkley (Ed.), Attention Deficit Hyperactivity Disorder: A handbook for diagnosis and treatment (pp. 540-572). New York: Guilford Press.

126. Kendall, P. C., Ronan, K. R., & Epps, J. (1991). Aggression in children/adolescents: Cognitive-behavioral treatment perspectives. In D. J. Peplar & K. H. Rubin (Eds.), The development and treatment of childhood aggression (pp. 341-360). Hillsdale, NJ: Lawrence Erlbaum Associates.

127. Feldman, R. A., & Caplinger, T. E. (1983). The St. Louis experiment: Treatment of antisocial youths in prosocial peer groups. In J. R. Kluegel (Ed.), Evaluating juvenile justice (pp. 121-148). Beverly Hills, CA: Sage.

128. Catterall, J. S. (1987). An intensive group counseling dropout prevention intervention: Some cautions on isolating at-risk adolescents within high schools. American Education Research Journal, 24, 521-540.

129. Dishion, T. J., & Andrews, D. W. (1995). Prevention escalation in problem behaviors with high-risk young adolescents: Immediate and 1-year outcome. Journal of Consulting and Clinical Psychology, 63, 538-548.

130. Lochman, J. E., Burch, P. R., Curry, J. F., & Lampon, L. B. (1984). Treatment and generalization effects of cognitive-behavioral and goal-setting interventions with aggressive boys. Journal of Consulting and Clinical Psychology, 52, 915-916.

131. Oden, S., & Asher, S. R. (1977). Coaching children in social skills training for friendship making. Child Development, 48, 495-506.

132. Ladd, G. W. (1981). Effectiveness of a social learning method for enhancing children's social interaction and peer acceptance. Child Development, 52, 171-178.

133. Kendall, P. C., Kane, M., Howard, B., & Siqueland, L. (1989). Cognitive-behavioral therapy for anxious children: Treatment manual. Available from the author, Department of Psychology, Temple University, Philadelphia, PA 19122.

134. Meichenbaum, D. H., & Goodman, J. (1971). Training impulsive children to talk to themselves as a way of developing self-control. Journal of Abnormal Child Psychology, 77, 115-126.

135. Taylor, T. K., Eddy, J. M., & Biglan, A. (1999). Interpersonal skills training to reduce aggressive and delinquent behavior. Limited evidence and the need for an evidence-based system of care. Clinical Child and Family Psychology Review, 2, 169-182.

136. Kazdin, Esveldt-Dawson, French, & Unis, 1987). Effects of parent management and problem-solving skills training combined in the treatment of child antisocial behavior. Journal of the American Academy of Child and Adolescent Psychiatry, 26, 416-424.

137. Kendall, P. C., Reber, M., McCleer, S., Epps, J., & Ronan, K. R. (1990). Cognitive-behavioral treatment of conduct disordered children. Cognitive Therapy and Research, 14, 279-297.

138. Kazdin, A. E., Esveldt-Dawson, K., French, N. H., & Unis, A. S. (1987). Problem-solving skills training and relationship therapy in the treatment of antisocial child behavior. Journal of Consulting and Clinical Psychology, 55, 76-85.

139. Derzon, J. H., & Lipsey, M. W. (2000). Family features and problem, aggressive, criminal, or violent behavior: A meta-analytic inquiry. Manuscript submitted for publication.

140. Walsh, W. M. (1980). A primer in family therapy. Springfield, IL: Charles C. Thomas.

141. Alexander, J. F. (1973). Defensive and supportive communications in normal and deviant families. Journal of Consulting and Clinical Psychology, 40, 223-231.

142. Kazdin, A. E. (1985). Treatment of antisocial behavior in children and adolescents. Homewood, IL: Dorsey Press.

143. Jacob, T. (1975). Family interaction in disturbed and normal families: A methodological and substantive review. Psychological Bulletin, 82, 33-65.

144. Jacob, T. (Ed.) (1987). Family interaction and psychopathology: Theories, methods, & findings. New York: Plenum Press.

145. Bateson, G., Jackson, D. D., Haley, J., & Weakland, J. (1956). Toward a theory of schizophrenia. Behavioral Science, 1, 251-264.

146. Alexander, J. F., & Parsons, B. V. (1973). Short-term behavioral intervention with delinquent families: Impact on family process and recidivism. Journal of Abnormal Psychology, 81, 219-225.

147. Klein, N. C., Alexander, J. F., & Parsons, B. V. (1977). Impact of family systems intervention on recidivism and sibling delinquency: A model of primary prevention and program evaluation. Journal of Consulting and Clinical Psychology, 45, 469-474.

148. Alexander, J. F., Waldron, H. B., Newberry, A. M., & Liddle, N. (1988). Family approaches to treating delinquents. In E. W. Nunnally, C. S. Chilman, & F. M. Cox (Eds.), Mental illness, delinquency, addictions, and neglect. Newbury Park, CA: Sage.

149. Henggeler, S. W. (1990). Family therapy and beyond: A multisystemic approach to treating the behavior problems of children and adolescents. Pacific Grove, CA: Brooks/Cole.

150. Randall, J., & Henggeler, S. W. (1999). Multisystemic therapy: Changing the social ecologies of youths presenting serious clinical problems and their families. In S. Walker Russ, & T. H. Ollendick (Eds.), Handbook of psychotherapies with children and families, Issues in clinical child psychology (pp. 405-418). New York: Kluwer Academic/Plenum.

151. Bourdin, C. M., Mann, B. J., Cone, L., Henggeler, S. W., Fucci, B. R., Blaske, D. M., & Williams, R. A. (1992). Multisystemic treatment of adolescents referred for serious and repeated antisocial behavior. Unpublished manuscript, Medical University of South Carolina, Charleston.

152. Henggeler, S. W., Melton, G. B., & Smith, L. A. (1992). Family preservation using multisystemic therapy: An effective alternative to incarcerating serious juvenile offenders. Journal of Consulting and Clinical Psychology, 60, 953-961.

153. Henggeler, S. W. (1993, February). Family preservation using multisystemic treatment: A cost-savings strategy for reducing recidivism and institutionalization of serious juvenile offenders. Paper presented at the fifth annual meeting of the Society for Research in Child and Adolescent Psychopathology, Sante Fe, NM.

154. Feldman, R. A. (1992). The St. Louis experiment: Effective treatment of antisocial youths in prosocial peer groups. In J. McCord & R. E. Tremblay (Eds.), Preventing antisocial behavior (pp. 232-252). New York: Guilford Press.

155. Pelham, W. E., & Hoza, B. (1993, February). Comprehensive treatment for ADHD: A proposal for intensive summer treatment programs and outpatient follow-up. Paper presented at the fifth annual meeting of The Society for Research in Child and Adolescent Psychopathology. Santa Fe, NM.

156. Arnold, L. E., Abikoff, H. B., Cantwell, D. P., Conners, C. K., Elliott, G. R., Greenhill, L. L., Hechtman, L., Hinshaw, S. P., Hoza, B., Jensen, P. S., Kraemer, H. C., March, J. S., Newcorn, J. H., Pelham, W. E., Richters, J. E., Schiller, E., Severe, J. B., Swanson, J. M., Vereen, D., Wells, K. C. (1997). NIMH collaborative multimodal treatment study of children with ADHD (MTA): Design, methodology, and protocol evolution. Journal of Attention Disorders, 2(3), 141-158.

157. Richters J. E., Arnold, L. E., Jensen, P. S., Abikoff, H., et. al. (1995). NIMH collaborative multisite multimodal treatment study of children with ADHD: I. Background and rationale. Journal of the American Academy of Child & Adolescent Psychiatry, 34(8), 987-1000.

158. Jensen P. S. (1999). Fact versus fancy concerning the multimodal treatment study for attention-deficit hyperactivity disorder. Canadian Journal of Psychiatry, 44(10), 975-980.

159. Multimodal Treatment Study of Children with ADHD Cooperative Group US. (1999). A 14-month randomized clinical trial of treatment strategies for attention-deficit/hyperactivity disorder. Archives of General Psychiatry, 56(12), 1073-1086.

160. Pelham, W. E., Jr. (1999). The NIMH multimodal treatment study for attention-deficit hyperactivity disorder: Just say yes to drugs alone? Canadian Journal of Psychiatry, 44(10), 981-990.

161. Boyle, M. H. & Jadad, A.R. (1999). Lessons from large trials: The MTA study as a model for evaluation the treatment of childhood psychiatric disorder. Canadian Journal of Psychiatry, 44 (10), 991-998.

162. Cunningham, C. E. (1999). In the wake of the MTA: Charting a new course for the study and treatment of children with attention-deficit hyperactivity disorder. Canadian Journal of Psychiatry, 44(10), 999-1006.

163. Main, M., Kaplan, N., & Cassidy, J. (1985). Security in infancy, childhood, and adulthood: A move to the level of representation. IN I. Bretherton & E. Waters (Eds.), Growing points of attachment theory and research. Monographs of the Society for Research in Child Development, 50 (1-2, Serial No. 209).

164. Bowlby, J. (1973). Attachment and loss: Vol. 2. Separation. New York: Basic Books.

165. Sroufe, L. A., & Flesson, J. (1986). Attachment and the construction of relationships. In W. Hartup & Z. Rubin (Eds.), Relationships and development (pp. 51-71). Hillsdale, NJ: Lawrence Erlbaum Associates.

166. Speltz, M. L. (1990). The treatment of preschool conduct problems: An integration of behavioral and attachment concepts. In M. T. Greenberg, D. Cicchetti, & M. Cummings (Eds.), Attachment in the preschool years: Theory, research, and intervention (pp. 399-426). Chicago: University of Chicago Press.

167. Cloninger, C. R., & Gottesman, I. I. (1987). Genetic and environmental factors in antisocial behavior disorders. In S. A. Mednick, T. E. Moffit, & S. A. Stack (Eds.), The causes of crime: New biological approaches (pp. 92-109). New York: Cambridge University Press.

168. Albert, D. J., Walsh, M. L., Jonik, R. H. (1994). Aggression in humans: What is its biological foundation? Neuroscience and Biobehavioral Reviews, 17, 405-425.

169. Hutchings, B., & Mednick, S. A. (1974). Registered criminality in the adoptive and biological parents of registered male criminal adoptees. In R. R. Frieve, D. Rosenthal, & H. Brill (Eds.), Genetic research in psychiatry. Baltimore: Johns Hopkins University Press.

170. Mednick, S. A., Gabrielli, W. F., & Hutchings, B. (1984). Genetic influences in criminal convictions: Evidence from an adoption cohort. Science, 224, 891-894.

171. Cadoret, R. J., Cain, C. A., Crowe, R. R. (1983). Evidence for gene-environment interaction in the development of adolescent antisocial behavior. <u>Behavior Genetics</u>, <u>13</u>, 301-310.

172. Bohman, M., Cloninger, C. R., Sigvardsoon, S., & von Knorring, A. (1982). Predisposition to petty criminality in Swedish adoptees: I. Genetic and environmental heterogeneity. <u>Archives of General Psychiatry</u>, <u>39</u>, 1233-1241.

173. Dalgard, O. S., & Kringlen, E. (1976). A Norwegian twin study of criminality. <u>British Journal of Criminology</u>, <u>16</u>, 213-232.

174. Bohman, M. (1978). Some genetic aspects of alcoholism and criminality. <u>Archives of General Psychiatry</u>, <u>35</u>, 269-276.

175. Loeber, R., Stouthamer-Loeber, M., & Green, S. M. (1991). Age of onset of problem behavior in boys and later disruptive and delinquent behavior. <u>Criminal Behavior and Mental Health</u>, <u>1</u>, 229-246.

176. Goodman, R., & Stevenson, J. (1989). A twin study of hyperactivity: II. The etiological role of genes, family relationships, and perinatal adversity. <u>Journal of Child Psychology and Psychiatry</u>, <u>30</u>, 691-709.

177. Fishbein, D. (2000). The importance of neurobiological research to the prevention of psychopathology. <u>Prevention Science</u>, <u>1</u>(2), 89-106.

178. Plomin, R., & Hershberger, S. (1991). Genotype-environment interaction. In T. D. Wachs & R. Plomin (Eds.), <u>Conceptualization and measurement of organism-environment interaction</u> (pp. 29-43). Washington, DC: American Psychological Association.

179. Safer, D. J., & Krager, J. M. (1988). A survey of medication treatment for hyperactive/inattentive students. <u>Journal of the American Medical Association</u>, <u>260</u>, 2256-2258.

180. Wilens, T. E., & Biederman, J. (1992). The stimulants. <u>Psychiatric Clinics of North America</u>, <u>15</u>, 191-222.

181. DuPaul, G. J., & Barkley, R. A. (1990). Medication therapy. In R. A. Barkley (Ed.), <u>Attention Deficit Hyperactivity Disorder: A handbook for diagnosis and treatment</u> (pp. 573-612). New York: Guilford Press.

182. Gadow, K. D. (1981). Prevalence of drug treatment for hyperactivity and other childhood behavior disorders. In K. D. Gadow & J. Loney (Eds.), <u>Psychosocial aspects of drug treatment for hyperactivity</u> (pp. 13-70). Boulder, CO: Westview Press.

183. Elia, J., Stoff, D. M., & Coccaro, E. F. (1992). Biological correlates of impulsive behavior disorders: Attention deficit hyperactivity disorder, conduct disorder, and borderline personality disorder. In E. Peschel, R. Peschel, C. W. Howe, & J. W. Howe (Eds.), <u>Neurobiological disorders in children and adolescents</u> (pp. 51-57). San Francisco, CA: Jossey-Bass.

184. Greenhill, L. L., (1992). Pharmacologic treatment of Attention Deficit Hyperactivity Disorder. <u>Psychiatric Clinics of North America</u>, <u>15</u>, 1-27.

185. Safer, D. J., & Allen, R. P. (1989). Absence of tolerance to the behavioral effects of methylphenidate in hyperactive and inattentive children. <u>Journal of Pediatrics</u>, <u>115</u>, 1003-1008.

186. Pelham, W. E., & Hoza, J. (1987). Behavioral assessment of psychostimulant effects on ADD children in a summer day treatment program. In R. Prinz (Ed.), <u>Advances in behavioral assessment of children and families</u> (Vol. 3, pp. 3-33). Greenwich, CT: JAI Press.

187. Pelham, W. E., & Milich, R. (1991). Individual differences in response to Ritalin in classwork and social behavior. In L. Greenhill & B. P. Osman (Eds.), <u>Ritalin: Theory and management</u> (pp. 203-221). New York: MaryAnn Liebert, Inc.

188. Hoza, B., Vallano, G., & Pelham, W. E. (1995). Attention-deficit /hyperactivity disorder. In R. T. Ammerman & M. Hersen (Eds.), <u>Handbook of child behavior therapy in the psychiatric setting</u> (pp. 181-198). New York: John Wiley & Sons.

189. Pelllham, W.E., Carlson, C., Sams S. E.., Vallano, G., Dixon, M. J., and Hoza, B. (1993). Separate and combined effects of methylphenidate and behavior modification on boys with attention deficit hyperactivity disorder in the classroom. <u>Journal of Consulting and Clinical Psychology</u>, <u>61(3)</u>, 506-515.

190. Barkley, R. A. (1977). A review of stimulant drug research with hyperactive children. <u>Journal of Child Psychology and Psychiatry</u>, <u>18</u>, 137-165.

191. Gittelman, K. (1987). Pharmacotherapy of childhood hyperactivity: An update. In Meltzer, H. Y. (Ed.), Psychopharmacology: The third generation of progress (pp. 1215-1224). New York: Raven.

192. Sprague, R. L., & Sleator, E. K. (1977). Methylphenidate in hyperkinetic children: Differences in dose effects on learning and social behavior. Science, 198, 1274-1276.

193. Campbell, M., Small, A. M., Green, W. H., et al. (1984). Behavioral efficacy of haloperidol and lithium carbonate: A comparison in hospitalized aggressive children with conduct disorder. Archives of General Psychiatry, 41, 650-656.

194. Whitaker, A., & Rao, U. (1992). Neuroleptics in pediatric psychiatry. Psychiatric Clinics of North America, 15, 243-276.

195. Greenhill, L. L., (1992). Pharmacologic treatment of Attention Deficit Hyperactivity Disorder. Psychiatric Clinics of North America, 15, 1-27.

196. Gittelman, K. (1987). Pharmacotherapy of childhood hyperactivity: An update. In Meltzer, H. Y. (Ed.), Psychopharmacology: The third generation of progress (pp. 1215-1224). New York: Raven.

197. Jacobvitz, D., Srouge, L. A., Stewart, M. et al. (1991). Treatment of attentional and hyperactivity problems in children with sympathomimetic drugs: A comprehensive review. Journal of the American Academy of Child and Adolescent Psychiatry, 29, 677-688.

We Want Your Opinion!

Comments about the book: _____

Name of Book

_____

_____

_____

_____

Other titles you want Compact Clinicals to offer:

_____

_____

_____

_____

Please provide your name and address in the space below to be placed on our mailing list.

_____

_____

_____

_____

Compact Clinicals

Ordering in three easy steps:

1 **Please fill out completely:**

Billing/Shipping Information

Individual/Company   Department/Mail Stop

Profession

Street Address/P.O. Box

City, State, Zip

Telephone   ☐ Ship to residence   ☐ Ship to business

2 **Here's what I'd like to order:**

Book Name	Book Qty.	Unit Price	Total
Aggressive and Defiant Behavior The Latest Assessment and Treatment Strategies for the Conduct Disorders		$14.95	
Attention Deficit Hyperactivity Disorder (in Adults and Children) The Latest Assessment and Treatment Strategies		$14.95	
Borderline Personality Disorder The Latest Assessment and Treatment Strategies		$14.95	
Depression in Adults The Latest Assessment and Treatment Strategies		$14.95	
Obsessive Compulsive Disorder The Latest Assessment and Treatment Strategies		$14.95	
Post-Traumatic Stress Disorder The Latest Assessment and Treatment Strategies		$14.95	
		Subtotal	
		Tax Add (6.85% in MO)	
		Shipping Fee Add ($3.75 for the first book and $1.00 for each additional book)	
		Total Amount	

Continuing Education credits available for mental health professionals.
Call 1-800-408-8830 for details.

3 **Payment Method:** Telephone Orders/Toll Free: 1(800)408-8830 • Fax Orders to: 1(816)587-7198
Send Postal Orders to: Compact Clinicals • 7205 NW Waukomis Dr., Suite A • Kansas City, MO   64151
☐ Check Enclosed
☐ Please charge to my:
○ Visa   Name on Card
○ MasterCard   Cardholder Signature
○ Discover Card   Account #/Exp. Date _ _ _ _ - _ _ _ _ - _ _ _ _ - _ _ _ _ (_ _/_ _)

We Want Your Opinion!

Comments about the book: _____
Name of Book

_____

_____

_____

_____

Other titles you want Compact Clinicals to offer:

_____

_____

_____

_____

Please provide your name and address in the space below to be placed on our mailing list.

_____

_____

_____

_____

Compact Clinicals

Ordering in three easy steps:

1 **Please fill out completely:**

Billing/Shipping Information

Individual/Company _____ Department/Mail Stop _____

Profession _____

Street Address/P.O. Box _____

City, State, Zip _____

Telephone _____ ☐ Ship to residence   ☐ Ship to business

2 **Here's what I'd like to order:**

Book Name	Book Qty.	Unit Price	Total
Aggressive and Defiant Behavior The Latest Assessment and Treatment Strategies for the Conduct Disorders		$14.95	
Attention Deficit Hyperactivity Disorder (in Adults and Children) The Latest Assessment and Treatment Strategies		$14.95	
Borderline Personality Disorder The Latest Assessment and Treatment Strategies		$14.95	
Depression in Adults The Latest Assessment and Treatment Strategies		$14.95	
Obsessive Compulsive Disorder The Latest Assessment and Treatment Strategies		$14.95	
Post-Traumatic Stress Disorder The Latest Assessment and Treatment Strategies		$14.95	
		Subtotal	
		Tax Add (6.85% in MO)	
		Shipping Fee Add ($3.75 for the first book and $1.00 for each additional book)	
		Total Amount	

Continuing Education credits available for mental health professionals. Call 1-800-408-8830 for details.

3 **Payment Method:** Telephone Orders/Toll Free: 1(800)408-8830 • Fax Orders to: 1(816)587-7198
Send Postal Orders to: Compact Clinicals • 7205 NW Waukomis Dr., Suite A • Kansas City, MO 64151

☐ Check Enclosed
☐ Please charge to my:

◯ Visa   Name on Card _____

◯ MasterCard   Cardholder Signature _____

◯ Discover Card Account #/Exp. Date _ _ _ _ - _ _ _ _ - _ _ _ _ - _ _ _ _ (_ _/_ _)

We Want Your Opinion!

Comments about the book: _____

Name of Book

_____

_____

_____

_____

Other titles you want Compact Clinicals to offer:

_____

_____

_____

_____

Please provide your name and address in the space below to be placed on our mailing list.

_____

_____

_____

_____

Ordering in three easy steps:

1 **Please fill out completely:**

Billing/Shipping Information

Individual/Company _____ Department/Mail Stop _____

Profession _____

Street Address/P.O. Box _____

City, State, Zip _____

Telephone _____ ☐ Ship to residence ☐ Ship to business

2 **Here's what I'd like to order:**

Book Name	.	Book Qty.	Unit Price	Total
Aggressive and Defiant Behavior The Latest Assessment and Treatment Strategies for the Conduct Disorders			$14.95	
Attention Deficit Hyperactivity Disorder (in Adults and Children) The Latest Assessment and Treatment Strategies			$14.95	
Borderline Personality Disorder The Latest Assessment and Treatment Strategies			$14.95	
Depression in Adults The Latest Assessment and Treatment Strategies			$14.95	
Obsessive Compulsive Disorder The Latest Assessment and Treatment Strategies			$14.95	
Post-Traumatic Stress Disorder The Latest Assessment and Treatment Strategies			$14.95	

Subtotal	
Tax Add (6.85% in MO)	
Shipping Fee Add ($3.75 for the first book and $1.00 for each additional book)	
Total Amount	

Continuing Education credits available for mental health professionals. Call 1-800-408-8830 for details.

3 **Payment Method:** Telephone Orders/Toll Free: 1(800)408-8830 • Fax Orders to: 1(816)587-7198

Send Postal Orders to: Compact Clinicals • 7205 NW Waukomis Dr., Suite A • Kansas City, MO 64151

☐ Check Enclosed

☐ Please charge to my:

○ Visa   Name on Card _____

○ MasterCard   Cardholder Signature _____

○ Discover Card   Account #/Exp. Date _ _ _ _ - _ _ _ _ - _ _ _ _ - _ _ _ _   (_ _/_ _)

We Want Your Opinion!

Comments about the book: _____

Name of Book

_____

_____

_____

_____

Other titles you want Compact Clinicals to offer:

_____

_____

_____

Please provide your name and address in the space below to be placed on our mailing list.

_____

_____

_____

_____

Compact Clinicals

Ordering in three easy steps:

1 **Please fill out completely:**

Billing/Shipping Information

Individual/Company   Department/Mail Stop

Profession

Street Address/P.O. Box

City, State, Zip

Telephone   ☐ Ship to residence   ☐ Ship to business

2 **Here's what I'd like to order:**

Book Name	Book Qty.	Unit Price	Total
Aggressive and Defiant Behavior The Latest Assessment and Treatment Strategies for the Conduct Disorders		$14.95	
Attention Deficit Hyperactivity Disorder (in Adults and Children) The Latest Assessment and Treatment Strategies		$14.95	
Borderline Personality Disorder The Latest Assessment and Treatment Strategies		$14.95	
Depression in Adults The Latest Assessment and Treatment Strategies		$14.95	
Obsessive Compulsive Disorder The Latest Assessment and Treatment Strategies		$14.95	
Post-Traumatic Stress Disorder The Latest Assessment and Treatment Strategies		$14.95	

	Subtotal	
	Tax Add (6.85% in MO)	
	Shipping Fee Add ($3.75 for the first book and $1.00 for each additional book)	
	Total Amount	

Continuing Education credits available for mental health professionals.
Call 1-800-408-8830 for details.

3 **Payment Method:** Telephone Orders/Toll Free: 1(800)408-8830 • Fax Orders to: 1(816)587-7198
Send Postal Orders to: Compact Clinicals • 7205 NW Waukomis Dr., Suite A • Kansas City, MO 64151
☐ Check Enclosed
☐ Please charge to my:
     ○ Visa   Name on Card
     ○ MasterCard   Cardholder Signature
     ○ Discover Card   Account #/Exp. Date   _ _ _ _ - _ _ _ _ - _ _ _ _ - _ _ _ _   (_ _ / _ _)